THIS LITTLE PIGGY

THIS LITTLE PIGGY

NAN WELBURN

TEMPLE PUBLISHING COMPANY
London, England

First published in Great Britain 1996
by Temple Publishing Company
Edinburgh House, 19 Nassau Street
London W1N 7RE

Copyright © Nan Welburn 1996

British Library Cataloguing-in-Publication Data.
A catalogue record for this book is available
from the British Library.

ISBN 1 85977 071 1

Cover design Harold King

Photosetting by Keyboard Services, Luton, Beds
Printed and bound in England by
Intype London Ltd

DEDICATED
to the Memory
of
the Most Wonderful Woman in the World,
– MY MOTHER –

All my past Life is mine no more,
The flying hours are gone:
Like transitory Dreams giv'n o'er,
Whose images are kept in store
    By Memory alone.
                              ROCHESTER

We have always wanted a 'bit of land in Yorkshire' – a piece
whereon we could stand and look around and say 'All this is
ours!' Now we own such a 'bit' in the North Yorkshire National
Park, but it is quite a long story...
    It all began when we were home on leave from Sarawak in

1954
SPRING

March
The children are in need of roots and what better than roots in
the soil. We have decided to look for a smallholding, big
enough to keep pigs and poultry. I don't care how remote it is,
but plumbing is an absolute 'must' with me – village pumps

1

at the end of the village street are very picturesque – but – and, remembering the 'little house' down the garden of my youth, no!

It's quite a shock to come back and find two enormous beings towering above me, instead of the children we left almost three years ago. Granny has done a good job on them in the holidays and they certainly haven't suffered from school food. David J, 16 now, tall and athletic, 880-yards champion. Can he be the same boy as the three-year-old who was so concerned about the fate of 'Poor Nelly Gray', so many years ago? 'Will they ever bring her back, Mummy?' he asked tearfully, as I soulfully 'had-her-taken-away'. Then there is Vivienne Carole, almost 13, dwarfing me by at least four inches, witty and clever, writing poetry, and getting it in the school mag. Is she the same as the little girl who left her sandals near the deep pond as she wanted to paddle because the ducks did? I think so, she is still either up in the clouds in absolute raptures or down in the depths in the dumps. Granny is wonderful, a sprightly young-at-heart 76, but too old to take the children for the holidays again. After all, she has had her share of children, bringing up nine out of ten. Still, I think my two have kept her alive, as she might have moped after Dad died; at least I am making this an excuse to myself for having put on her. I think she enjoyed it really, but now she's thinking of giving up her home and living amongst us.

All normal leave activities must be subordinated in our search for a suitable place.

April

We have collected the children for the Easter holidays and are scanning all the local newspapers for adverts. Have visited Harwood Dale, Rosedale and lots of other dales, even crossed the Humber on the Ferry to New Holland. There are too many snags – some places are too large, some too small and some – no plumbing. We are decorating our little house with a view to selling, when we find a suitable property, and it is beginning to look very nice.

Wednesday 14th

Think we have spotted it. It certainly sounds promising, 26 acres, house with four bedrooms, two sitting rooms, study, two bathrooms, three WCs, h & c, Aga Cooker, calor gas etc. Enough plumbing there to satisfy even me. We rang up the agent and he told us the key was with Mrs B. in Kilburn, the nearest village. The place had been a Fox Farm at one time and the present owner bred greyhounds when he lived there, but it hasn't really been farmed for years. No harm in looking, although it will strain the old bank balance a bit.

Thursday 15th

A lovely April day – a lovely ride in the Zephyr to a pretty little village. Kilburn is guarded by The White Horse which can be seen for miles on the Hambleton Hills. Mrs B. was out, but we decided to have a look at the place anyway, when we had come so far. We asked the way of a man working in his garden nearby. 'Tak t'fost leeane on t'left efter t'signpost to High Kilburn, but deean't tak yon posh car up t'ill, there's a rum corner hauf way up.' Following his directions and advice, we left the car at the bottom and set off up the lane. The primroses were peeping out from under the hedgerows like little yellow fairies. We were entranced; Vivienne simply had to pick some. It was uphill all the way. Coming to the 'rum' corner, we saw a van parked in the side of the lane. Clearly it had 'refused'. There was loose grit on the road surface, which certainly wouldn't help.

On we went, beginning to tire a little; it seemed a long way but, at least, Vivienne was getting some exercise. At last we came to a gate with the words 'Hambleton Fox Farm' faintly discernible on it, no sign of a farm or of any sort of dwelling of any description, nothing but a glorious view, and some old wire pens in the field. 'It can't be far now, surely,' I encouraged. Another 200 yards and the chimneys came into view; it was quite fascinating to see the house appear gradually as we came over the rise! Like building a house in reverse from chimneys to foundation. Daffodils were waving in the field, as we stood and looked. There it was – a solid stone-built house, facing south, with a long roof sloping right down to the ground floor at the back. All the emphasis is on the front,

3

and the large sitting room has a window at the side and a big bay at the front, so it will get the sun all day (when there is sun).

We couldn't get in, so had to content ourselves with peering in through the windows. I like the look of the house very much and, of course, the plumbing weighs very heavily in its favour. There is a very steep bank rising up from the back of the house towering above it protectingly, and at the top, on the skyline, three Scots pines, very noble and magnificent in their loneliness. On the western side is a field, then an avenue of trees bordering a brook; the catkins hang like lambs' tails. Rising from the brook is the White Horse hill, but the Horse is not visible from this side. A house like this, in a more accessible position, would be worth much more than they are asking. The study ceiling is down; all the plaster has fallen off; there must have been a burst pipe. It hasn't been occupied for about a year and is in rather a neglected condition, but that can easily be remedied. It looks lonely and appealing. From our short inspection, the outbuildings seem in reasonable condition; a stone-built garage and shed, with barn behind; a tarred wooden stable and cowhouse and four boxes or pens, brick-built, of fairly recent erection, snuggling in at the bottom of the steep bank. In front of the house is a derelict garden and a big field; to the side, more broken-down sheds and rusty wire, showing here and there among the fresh green nettles.

Rabbits abound, and the tender green knuckles of bracken are pushing through the bank. It is altogether a delightful spot. We are getting quite excited about it, and must show it to David on Sunday.

Sunday 18th
Vivienne is 13 today and Granny is staying with us. We took David to see the house, promising to be back in time for the birthday tea. David liked the look of it at first sight. The weather was lovely; the sun shone out of a cloudless blue sky, the air wax clear and, what was more, there were millions, well – not quite millions, but hundreds of rabbits, and he could imagine himself walking over the fields with a gun and a dog. We didn't walk up, but risked the 'rum' corner. The Zephyr, driven, of course, by an expert, managed it, skidding

4

a little it must be confessed, but saving us that long walk. The agent has told us that the study ceiling will be repaired and, something we didn't know, there are ten acres of moorland and four acres of grass, on top of the bank. I have no idea of acreage at all, and would never have guessed it, but this adds to its attraction. We had the key this time and explored the house from top to bottom; it has been used in two parts, the back part being used by the servants and the front by the master of the house. The back door opens into the scullery with an Aga cooker and a sink; to the right a door opens into a bathroom and WC and straight through is the living-room kitchen, off which is a large room, presumably the bedroom. Quite a self-contained flat. An excellent pantry, facing north, leads out of the kitchen. The front part of the house is very spacious. The kitchen door opens into an L-shaped hall, the passage to the left, with hooks on the wall, ending with a WC and the other arm of the L leading to the front door. A wide staircase faces the front door, and at the bottom of the stairs a door opens into the big room – a sunny room indeed. On the other side of the hall is the little sitting room and the study. There are three bedrooms upstairs, a large one over the large downstairs room, and two smaller ones over the small room and study, all with wash basins, h & c; then a bathroom with WC and a cylinder cupboard, very spacious, with a trapdoor leading to the loft, and a large sloping-roofed attic over the kitchen. It is like a palace; I am thrilled with it, although we shan't have enough furniture to furnish it properly. Hot and cold water in the bedrooms, two bathrooms and three lavatories, what heaven! Twenty-six acres is all very nice, but plumbing!

There is a power house, built of wood, in the shed, housing an engine which makes electricity, and batteries for storage. The engine looks in very poor condition, even to me. In the tarred shed are stalls for two cows, a loose box and a large stable; the four brick-built boxes have been used as kennels. We decide that, if we can get a reasonable mortgage, we will have it, and, in great excitement, return home once more. I am afraid we were a little late for tea, but our excitement overrode all disappointment, and we tossed prospective names to and fro across the tea table. We couldn't call it

5

'Hambleton Fox Farm', we didn't like it, and there haven't been foxes there for years, at least, not silver foxes. Something to do with the bracken. At last we had it, 'Bracken Hill'. This seems to give the place character. We are full of plans now.

The children have returned to school for the summer term.

May
A mortgage has been arranged with the building society. The study roof repair is being put in hand, our little house is being put up for sale and things are moving. On the conveyance the name is being changed to Bracken Hill, and the barometer is Set Fair.

Sunday 9th
A momentous day! Granny has her first glimpse of Bracken Hill. She liked it at first sight, but is not blind to the work involved. Intensely practical and interested, she explored it all, and really enjoyed the ride there and back. She is staying with us now, as it is lonely in her little cottage. I can see she will have to give it up, but it is a hard decision to make, as it has been her home for over 50 years. We have found an easier way to Bracken Hill, which enables us to avoid the 'rum' corner. We turn off near the Hambleton Hotel on the Helmsley-Thirsk road, as though to the Yorkshire Gliding Club then, instead of taking the right fork, we carry on straight down and there we are – much easier.

Friday 14th
Met Georgie at York station. She has come from Wales, where she is teaching now. Haven't seen her since she left Sarawak. We talked until two o'clock in the morning.

Saturday 15th
It is Vivienne's going-out weekend. We collected her from Hunmanby, went out to lunch, and then had a ride up Olivers Mount. This is the first time I have ever been up the mount, and I have lived round here practically all my life. It's quite true to say the visitor sees more than the resident. The view of the bay from the top is lovely and I wouldn't have missed it.

6

My schooldays were spent in the shadow of the mount. It dominates the view, equally with the castle, but at least I have seen the Castle, and written a composition about it too. What a lot Oliver Cromwell has to answer for!

To round off a lovely day, we went to the Opera House and saw a play, then returned Vivienne to school, arranging to call for her after morning chapel tomorrow.

Sunday 16th
Called for Vivienne, had lunch and then took Georgie to see Bracken Hill. We are like children with a new toy, everyone must see it. The sun shone, our spirits were high and Georgie duly admired our new acquisition. We had left it rather late for catching her train, so had an awful dash. Rounding corners on two wheels, we did the 30 miles to York station in record time, and caught the train. I don't like going at such speeds, especially on narrow country lanes, but Daddy enjoyed it. He's an excellent driver, that goes without saying. We returned V.C. to school and stayed to community hymn singing. I do enjoy singing.

Monday 17th
We seem to get all our visitors together, Barry and Penny are on leave too, and on their way to Scotland, so they are breaking their journey here. We went to meet them and Barry let me drive his new Anglia for the last 20 miles. It's just like old times.

Tuesday 18th
A lovely day again. We took Barry and Penny out to see Bracken Hill, and it was duly admired. Barry took some photographs, and Penny remarked that she thought it would involve a lot of work. We finished off by having tea at Byland Abbey Inn and had great fun with a very large dog. I love dogs.

Wednesday 19th
Went to York to see the minster. We see much more of the countryside when we are showing people around. I haven't been round the minster for years, but I am always very impressed.

Thursday 20th
Another lovely day, which we spent driving round the lovely Yorkshire lanes, finishing up with tea at the Raven Hall Hotel. What a lovely commanding view it has!

Friday 21st
Barry and Penny left for Scotland. We have had a lovely holiday with them, and would probably have been working like mad if they hadn't been here. I think the relaxation has been good for us. Arthur is on leave too, and is going to Norway. He will stay with us one night on his way to Newcastle to catch his ship. We went to York to meet him and took him round by Bracken Hill, no one can escape. Arthur thought it rather isolated, and wasn't envious, although he said the view was magnificent. I feel a proprietary right over the view, it is mine! As Arthur has to leave very early in the morning, I mustn't forget to set the alarm. I can't wake up without its aid.

22nd–31st
Daddy has gone off on a course. Somehow I always think of him as Daddy, because we called David after him, and it is terribly muddling. Now I am left with the job of selling the house. People come and people go, poking into every nook and cranny.

Granny has finally decided to give up her cottage. She is staying with me for the present. The little house looks very attractive in its new coat of paint. It is a sunny house. I think I have found a purchaser for it, for which I am truly thankful, although it will be rather a wrench to part with it. It was our first home, and we have been very happy here. Barry and Penny are calling on their way back, I had a letter from them today.

June

Thursday 3rd
Barry and Penny came back; the weather is absolutely glorious still. We made one more trip to Bracken Hill and Daddy and Barry went shooting, while Penny and I just sat and enjoyed

8

the view. They shot three rabbits. As it was getting late when we left, we bought some fish and chips in Helmsley, and ate them on the way home, out of the paper. How much nicer fish and chips taste out of the paper, in the right company, of course!

Friday 4th
We gave Barry and Penny a good send-off with all our good wishes and three rabbits, and then set off to Richmond for David, as it is his half-term. We just can't resist it, we had to call at Bracken Hill on our way back; it has a special magnetism. David shot two rabbits – now for rabbit pie.

5th–9th
Vivienne's half-term. The weather isn't too good, and there is always the odd bit of washing to be done. We have to take the children out too. All too soon, the weekend has slipped away and we have to take them both back. They do so enjoy being at home, it is a joy to have them.

Uncle D is bringing his big lorry over from Wales with an engine, which, according to him, will solve all our electricity problems at Bracken Hill. I certainly hope it will. We now have the key, and the immediate aim is to get the place cleaned up and ready for habitation. The plasterers have made a good job of the study ceiling, but a fine mess of the floor, and they have trampled white plaster all the way up the stairs, why? We haven't started the Aga yet, but we boil an old kettle on the kitchen fire and picnic. It is hard, dirty work, cleaning up, and scrubbing isn't my choice of jobs, but it must be done. At least the kitchen and scullery are easy, they are covered with lino.

The calor gas cylinder reposes in a wooden box, just beneath the kitchen window-sill. This supplies the kitchen and the sitting room with light. Footsteps echo hollowly through the emptiness.

Friday 11th
We spend all our time at Bracken Hill now. Uncle D and Harold, who came with him, and Daddy have been messing about with the engines all day, Harold nearly wearing himself

9

out turning the starting handle of the little one. The big one is housed in a little cubby-hole next to the coal-house, an excellent place for it; it just fits in and is out of the way. Uncle D eventually fixed it. The lights came on with a brilliancy which dazzled us, then – phut! – we were left in a blackness, darker than before. Now the engine won't rise to further heights and just sits there, very imposing, but as Granny says, 'Neither use nor ornament.' Attention is transferred to the little engine; it is started up and the batteries filled with juice. All this is completely out of my sphere, as I am no engineer.

12th–25th
We are rather unsettled, neither one thing nor another. As Granny has finally decided to give up her old home, she is sharing the things out among us. An excellent thing for us, as the furniture will help to fill the emptiness of Bracken Hill. Our little bit of furniture will be completely swallowed up. What a business this buying and selling is. I don't like moving, it involves such a lot, much more than just packing up clothes and going abroad. It means lifting out roots, and moving furniture and packing up everything. Still, we've done it now. My sister is coming up to help me to pack up. I feel very lethargic about it now that it has come to it.

Ida has come up to help pack up; she has just finished sorting out Granny's things at the cottage and our share is waiting to be collected by the removal van. It all fits in really, like a jigsaw puzzle.

We have sold the Zephyr and borrowed an old van from Uncle D. The garage rang up to say that we can now collect the new one. We also attended a farm sale, which we had seen advertised in the paper. These sales puzzle me, there only seems to be junk, but I suppose some of it is useful. We didn't buy anything, but it all adds up to experience.

SUMMER

June

Friday 25th

We removed to Bracken Hill. The removal van collected the furniture from Granny's cottage first, then packed our possessions in safely. Cups of tea, full instructions on how to get there, and they were off. We packed up the remainder of our things, the things we couldn't trust to the big van, and loaded up our old van and the new one. The house was very empty. We had weathered the war there; the children had been born in it, and now we were leaving it for good. It looked rather sad, and our feelings were mixed. We said our farewells and left.

We had burnt our boats!

We arrived at Bracken Hill shortly after the big van. The removers soon had the furniture dispersed. Dispersed is the word, because, even with Granny's bits and pieces, it is completely lost in this enormous house. We have made the big sitting room quite attractive, but the little one is empty except for Granny's old horsehair sofa. The study is empty too, except for the sewing machine and the telephone, a strange combination. The kitchen is very liveable; Granny's old dresser just fits on one wall. A couple of old fashioned armchairs round the fireplace, and a table and chairs, complete the picture. I suppose the bedrooms aren't too bad, and upon a pinch, we could make the attic into a bedroom. Maybe it would be a good idea to take in children for the holidays, children whose parents are abroad. I must go into this, maybe advertise.

Our pièce de résistance is the hall. There, we have a camphorwood chest, and above it, on the wall, we have mounted two Dyak blowpipes, crossed very professionally, with the quiver for poison arrows between. Above hangs an enormous Borneo hat (used out there against sun and rain), and at one side a Dyak parang (which has taken Jap heads) and at the other, a Brunei sword, each in a decorated scabbard. I have stained the floor and carpeted it with the stair carpet from the other house. The carpet is much too narrow for those magnificent stairs. They will have to wait. Granny's old table just fits into the scullery, and the washing machine fits near the sink. Not that it will be much good. What a good thing I bought a 'Goblin' – at least it has an Acme wringer and not an electric one. I chose it because the lid becomes a clothes basket; what funny reasons we women have for buying things! Not at all logical. It's a bit of luck Granny not having thrown away her old flat irons. These will be a godsend. All the other electrical equipment is now stored away in the cupboard under the stairs. Who knows? We may get it up here soon, electricity, I mean. That little white table looks at home in the upstairs bathroom. As Schoolboy Champion, 880 yards, David is representing the North Riding in the Yorkshire Championships at Beverley. I am sorry we couldn't go and watch him. Pity! We are so tired, I'm sure we'll sleep well in our new home.

Saturday 26th
Our first breakfast at Bracken Hill. We had slept well. Good thing we got the Aga going yesterday, the kettle boiled in a few minutes after being on the simmering plate all night. According to plan, the Welburn convoy set off across the Pennines to Wales, to collect our first stock and return the borrowed van. We have decided on Welsh pedigree pigs, after much thought, and will collect five weaners from a farm near to Uncle D's. The journey was uneventful, but as we were passing close to Daddy's sister Winnie's house, we called in for a cup of tea. Winnie is very interested in our enterprise. After the usual family gossip, we continued our journey, as we are staying the night with Uncle D.

Sunday 27th
Starting reasonably early, we went to the farm and collected five little pigs. What noisy things they are! The farmer had to be careful not to upset the mother. He weighed each one, and

the average weight is 38 lbs. We paid him £40 and set off for home with our first stock and a supply of meal sufficient to last until we could get some. We also collected two kittens from Uncle D's, tortoiseshell, which I call Torty, and a ginger, Kuning, which is the Malay word for yellow. With only one van this time, containing our precious cargo, we returned across the Pennines to the Hambleton Hills. The pigs are now installed in the stable and the kittens in the kitchen. As we have no fresh milk, they will just have to make do with tinned.

Monday 28th
Daddy has gone down to Thirsk for pig meal and poultry pellets. We have no poultry as yet, but they are next on the list.

I have sent off the advertisement for taking children in the holidays to the *Yorkshire Post*. They need references for this type of advert, very careful of them, and this has delayed things a bit. Anyway it's gone now, and I am wondering if there will be any replies.

Our nearest neighbour, Mr Binks, lives with his family, on a farm just over a mile away. His place is called High Farm, an odd name for it, as it is hidden away in a hollow, even more hidden than Bracken Hill, which can be seen from at least two vantage points in the village. I have been looking at the Ordnance Survey map; our house is called Bairns House on it, and Mr Binks' Hell Hole Barn, a much more descriptive name, I can't help thinking! We now get our milk from Mr Binks, until we get a cow. The Binks are very friendly and it is a long job getting a can of milk. I suppose they see so few people that they like to talk, when they get the chance. It's worth it for the fresh milk; I'm sick of tinned milk, so are the kittens.

Wednesday 30th
We have now started cleaning out the shed ready for deep-litter hens. It is hard, dirty work, but the results are good. It only remains to whitewash and then it will be ready for its occupants. Winnie knows of some point-of-lay pullets for sale near her. We tried to ring her up, but found the telephone was

out of order. Now what! A real technical hitch! Daddy decided to follow the lines down the woods and see if he could do anything about it, so off we went. It was like a jungle. Eventually we found a branch leaning on the wires. We had quite a job to 'unshort' or is it 'de-short' them? Anyway, when we got back, the telephone was in working order. Daddy rang up Winnie and arranged to go over and collect some pullets, going one day and coming back the next.

July

Friday 2nd
We have finished off the shed ready for the pullets. I have to stay at home, as we have stock now and we feel it better not to leave them, even though the pigs are feeding from a feeder which only needs refuelling every now and again, when it is empty, and the kittens aren't much trouble. I don't really like the idea of staying alone in this quiet spot very much. Daddy didn't go until late afternoon, and he will return as soon as he can. It is very, very quiet. The hills have withdrawn into themselves, under their blanket of green ferny fronds of bracken. Rabbits don't make any noise. I managed to keep myself busy until dusk, and now I am going to have a hot bath and go to bed early. I can almost feel the silence. We shall have to get a radio. Every little noise is magnified, and I find myself tiptoeing up the uncarpeted stairs. Am I a little frightened? I won't admit it, no! I won't!

Saturday 3rd
I must have slept last night, but I don't remember dropping off. Of course I was very tired and the fresh air and all that! Feeling very busy, I had breakfast, gave the kittens the last of the milk, had a look at the pigs to see if they were still there and, with a tin of creosote and a brush, I walked up the road to the gate. It was a lovely morning. How different things look in the light of day. The hills had expanded and now smiled down at me in the morning sunshine. Getting busy on the gate, I decided that when it was dry, I would christen us. The creosote soaked in very quickly, I don't suppose the gate had

ever had such a treat. Removing the old name, I screwed on the letters, bought from Woolworths some time before, BRACKEN HILL. As I have never been very good at getting-screws-going, this job took up a lot of my time, but it certainly looked good when it was finished, and I thought what a surprise it would be for my husband when he returned. Now I had to go across for some milk. Collecting all my tools, I returned home for the milk can, and set off to Old Binks', by this time we are calling him 'Old Binks'. Not that he is 'old' at all he is about our age, 41, strong and spare with a tanned face and very blue eyes, but it is an affectionate term, more than anything else. He talks with a very broad Yorkshire accent, which is very attractive to us, and being Yorkshire ourselves, is quite comprehensible.

Daddy got back safely with 75 pullets, Rhode Island Reds, at point-of-lay. They are lovely to look at, a deep golden brown. We put them in the shed with their deep litter and they settled down immediately.

Sunday 4th
A dreadful day, pouring with rain all day. Even the view forgotten, we hugged the fire only stirring to do the necessary chores. I decided to write letters; as I always write to the children weekly, what better time than a wet Sunday!

Monday 5th
Monday is market day in Thirsk. We haven't anything to take, as yet, but we have things to buy. Opening a bank account we transferred money from our Scarborough account. The manager was very accommodating, allowing us to draw on it right away. What trust! We felt good. Remembering the solitude of Bracken Hill, one of our purchases was an Ultra-Twin Radio set, which would run off batteries or mains electricity. We must, after all, keep in touch with what is happening in the outside world. Dropping in on the secretary of the NFU we had a long chat with him and joined the union. He was exceptionally nice and offered to help at any time. Our, purchases included a barrow, small enough for me to wheel, pig troughs, hen troughs and drinking fountains, a large zinc bucket and a white enamel milking pail. We also bought

15

special pig feeders, which just need filling up from time to time, and the pigs help themselves whenever they feel like it, which, from what I have seen already, is almost all the time. Greedy pigs maybe, but dirty pigs, no! They will never foul their bed, and have very clean habits, using a corner well away from the bed for a lavatory. Even the smallest obeys the rules and staggers across to the corner. A separator and a small hand churn, like a glass jar with a 'swizzle' in it, were deemed to be necessary and were included. I am going to have a bash at making butter.

Tuesday 6th
Daddy has been putting up a pen for the *Folies Bergères*, as we now call them, enclosing part of the bank. They love it and play hide and seek amongst the green ferny fronds of bracken. This will save cleaning out too, as they have transferred their corner outside.

We are still rather disorganised, as we have no equipment apart from what we have bought, and isn't that dear? Money is dwindling rapidly. Of course we have the tools which have survived our years abroad, mostly gardening tools, and the odd pair of pliers etc, and some which Granny has given us from Grandad's store, including a heavy fencing hammer, which Daddy has been wielding so professionally, and a muck fork and shovel.

I wonder when Old Binks will be able to cut the hay in the top four acres. It's ready and waiting, and he has promised to do it with his tractor and grass cutter.

Wednesday 7th
A lovely sunny day. Wash day too; I have to do the washing now to fit in with all my other activities. Old Binks, has, at last, cut the hay; I simply had to go and see. There it is, what is left of it after hundreds of rabbits have eaten their fill, lying in neat green swathes, just asking for the sun to shine on it and make it into our first crop of hay. How very nice new-mown hay smells!

We are making a hen run behind the house, with the wire from the dog pens; then we shall be able to watch these hens from the kitchen window.

Thursday 8th
Daddy rang up Winnie again and arranged to go over for some more pullets. I'm going this time; I don't like being left here by myself. We set off in the late afternoon, after seeing everything safely fastened up. I sometimes wonder why we go so far for our stock. There must surely be nearer places. Still I suppose that's how it is. Winnie is very interested, and the other hens are doing well; not quite laying but...

Friday 9th
Going to the farm where the other hens came from, we were entertained to lunch and made very welcome. Then we bought 75 more Rhode Islands, and were given two young cockerels, capons, for the table. Feeling very full, and grateful, we set off for home. On arrival, we found that two of our best pullets had been suffocated on the journey. It would be two pullets, and not the two cockerels, wouldn't it? They are hale and hearty and now have a reprieve, as we already have two corpses. How it hurts to lose something you have just paid for! Some of the hens we put in the deep-litter shed and the rest in the hen run. More beaks to feed.

Daddy's leave is coming to an end. I shall have to face it, we can't possibly afford this place without an income coming in regularly. What with school fees and the mortgage hanging over the homestead, it just can't be done. He will have to go abroad again. We have had many discussions on this subject, and have decided that I must try and build up the place, look after the stock, the children and the house, for at least a year, then we'll see. We have discussed this with Granny, and she insists on coming to stay with me after the summer holidays, when I shall be alone. It's rather a big thing to tackle! What alternative is there?

Have we bitten off more than we can chew?

Saturday 10th
Today is Vivienne's school garden party. I have missed this so often, I had to make a special effort, and she, wishing to make it difficult for me to get out of it, has put my name down for the Girls vs Mothers tennis. I haven't played for ages, and have had no practice at all since I came home. Too busy doing

17

other things. Play I must, whatever the cost. I hopped into the van, leaving Daddy in charge of the farm, and, collecting Granny from Ida's, arrived in plenty of time. Vivienne was very pleased to see us and, after changing into my very fetching short tennis skirt, I joined the other tennis-mothers and met my partner. She had had very little practice too, so we had very little hope of bringing off anything spectacular. However, we ran about energetically and did our noble best. What more can one do? The girls just beat us up, so, adding no glory, but having enjoyed our game, we watched the experts. Only one couple of Mums had any success. Still, everybody can't win, there must be losers, and who better than Mums. What lovely teas they make at Hunmanby! We enjoyed our tea very much, had a nice chat with Vivienne and her teachers, especially the Headmistress and, returning Granny to Ida's, I set off for home, meeting Daddy in the lane. He was rather tired of being on his own. What a lovely day I have had! So refreshing.

Monday 12th

The strongest memory is weaker than the palest ink.
Chinese Proverb

I have started to make lists to which I add. I just can't afford to forget anything. No little shop on the corner to run to, in an emergency. There must be no emergencies, so I have bought in a lot of provisions. The grocer in Thirsk is prepared to deliver once a week, which is a help. Enormous bills are rather frightening at first, but once I have a stock in, they won't be quite so high. Bought some cabbage plants, so we ought to have fresh veg at least. What's the use of living in the country if you have to buy veg? I cleared a small patch of land with difficulty, peeling off the grass with the rusty wire through which it had grown, and digging. The ground is very stony. What a paltry little square it looks! I've puddled the plants in too, so they ought to take. Finishing off by putting wire over the precious plants, I have visions of enormous-hearted cabbages.

Tuesday 13th
Our first egg – Daddy came in bearing it aloft as on a satin cushion. What excitement! Now who was to have it? We decided to wait for the next one, and then have one each. We feel like decorating the pullet which laid it. The sun has been pouring down all day and the hay needed turning. We went up into the hayfield. It was very peaceful, as we started with wooden rakes to turn the swathes over, then we decided hay forks were easier, but not much. What toil! Soon our faces were red with exertion, our arms weary and we were thoroughly sick of it. I looked at the field, four acres hadn't sounded very much, now it looked like a vast prairie. We struggled on. It was a case of 'the spirit's willing but the flesh is weak', or was the spirit even willing? I am beginning to think it wasn't. Teatime, we pounced on it as an excuse to stop, and, pouring with sweat (or do ladies only glow), we stumbled slowly down the hill and home. I made the tea, while Daddy fed the hens. Tea! magic word, we sat and relaxed, aching in every limb, at least I was, and Daddy looked as though he were too. Mechanisation of farming, I am all in favour. I must say the tea refreshed me, tea being the stimulant that it is, and I conjured up enough strength to wash up the pots.

'It's Kilburn Village Feast tonight,' observed Daddy, 'Old Binks told me; shall we go down and see what's doing?' 'Might as well,' I agreed, 'it will make a change.' So, having changed and smartened ourselves up a bit, we set off for the village. Whether it was that the sun had gone down, and it was slightly chilly, or whether it was that we were overtired, I don't know, probably a bit of both, but we just couldn't enter into the spirit of the thing. The fair and sports just didn't hold our attention, so we came home and went to bed.

My cabbages have gone; the beastly rabbits have had the lot!

Wednesday 14th
Half-day closing in Thirsk. We dashed down for some necessary shopping and bumped into Old Binks in the market square. 'Oh, golly, now we're for it,' I thought. We were. We gave him a lift back home, and stayed at his place talking. He has a beautiful little mule called Toby in the stable. I fell in love with him at first sight. 'Ah got 'im frae High Kilburn,' old Binks explained, 'Ah gev a quid for 'im.'

'I'll give you £2,' I offered quickly.

'Dun,' he replied, 'but Ah'd better keep 'im a lahtle bit longer, till Ah've brokken 'im in ti t'elter.' I agreed to wait but paid the £2 before he had time to change his mind. I am very thrilled at the thought of owning that dear little mule. The discussion then turned to bees. Bees were our wartime hobby, and we have always liked the busy creatures.

'Ah'll tell ya what Ah'll dae wi' ya,' he offered, 'Ah'll let ya 'ev yon box o' bees fer ten bob.' Ten shillings changed hands, and the box of bees, very industriously minding their own business, were ours. We have an empty hive, which we left with our former nextdoor neighbour. I now have visions of an apiary – row upon row of hives of busy bees, bringing in pounds and pounds of Yorkshire honey – and money. Isn't Vivienne a busy-bee or something at school? I have a headache. Is it the work or the tension?

Thursday 15th
Wash day! No electric washing machine to take all the drudgery out of washing, and allow the housewife to sit at the fireside with a good book. Oh no! I have to do things the hard way, the old posher in the dolly-tub first – not a dolly-stick, I just couldn't manage that. How Granny ever used to turn that thing, I don't know! Anyway a washing machine is really only a glorified dolly-stick, with the work taken out of it of course, which makes quite a difference. Rinsing in the sink (thank goodness for the Acme wringer), then with a straw clothes basket, which Granny gave me (I don't even use the Goblin lid), I go out into the clean fresh air and hang out the whiter-than-whites. No dirty, grimy washing for us. It smells so fresh and, after being ironed with the old flat irons heated on the Aga, is ready once more to be turned into 'dirty linen'. I don't really mind washing, if I have plenty of time and good weather, but what a ceaseless round is housework; sometimes I long for my Panchi*. But she wouldn't have been happy here, she would have been too cold.

---

* Panchi who was a Dyak was my servant in Miri Sarawak. She did the cooking and washing.

Friday 16th
Daddy's leave is nearing its end. His passport has gone off today to be checked and he has to have his inoculations. The tension is building up and he doesn't really want to go. But go he must, and we can't help it, 'What can't be cured, must be endured.' We must face it, we got ourselves into it and we must see it through. David has finished his GCEs. He has taken nine subjects, that seems an awful lot of subjects to me. I do hope he gets through, but I think he will. Wonder what he'll decide to be. He used to want to be a farmer. We'll see, after he has had a taste of it, or is this real farming? I'm inclined to think not.

Saturday 17th
The hens are laying now although we haven't enough eggs to take to market.

We decided to go and collect the beehive. Daddy has shot some rabbits. We take a couple and six of our precious eggs and set off, first of all to see Granny. She was thrilled with the eggs, as I knew she would be, and Ida was glad of the rabbit. We had animated discussions on everything under the sun, and, refreshed, sped on to swap the remaining rabbit for the beehive. A rabbit makes a change – a bit different from the time we were down in Tasmania where a whole field seemed to crawl with them. Daddy shot some then, and they were just thrown to the dogs. We haven't quite so many as that, but we have too many.

In our spare moments we have been cleaning out the cowhouse, and Daddy has made a very good job of white-washing it. We are rather tired of going over for the milk, and have decided to buy an attested cow. Attestation will be compulsory before long, so we must be attested. Have arranged for the Attestation Officer to come and pass our cowhouse.

Sunday 18th
It will soon be the school holidays. Busied myself getting the bedrooms ready. David will sleep in the small front one, which gets all the morning, sun. Vivienne will be next door, and we are using the large room opposite. There are two beds

in Vivienne's room, a small one under the window and an almost-double bed by the wall. Granny's feather bed is in the big one. This room is lovely in the afternoon, warm with sunshine and very cosy.

Cleared up my correspondence. We have joined the Yorkshire Pig Breeders' Association and the National Pig Breeders' Association.

Monday 19th
Although it is market day, we still haven't enough eggs to take to market, but we took the precaution of collecting an empty crate from the packing station van, just in case. We have decided to use the room next to the kitchen as an eggroom. Bought in lots of provisions for our two healthy youngsters, who have very large appetites.

The Attestation Officer came. Daddy proudly showed him the spotless cowhouse. 'This won't do at all,' he said, 'anything can be covered up with whitewash, it will all have to be scrubbed off.' Imagine, all that work for nothing, all that lovely whitewash has to be scrubbed off! We are devastated! No animal must be put in until he has passed it, and he will come again next week. We came in and put on the kettle. Nothing so heartening as a cup of tea – the cup that cheers...

Tuesday 20th
Set about scrubbing off the whitewash with soda in the water. My poor hands!

Wednesday 21st
Poor Daddy, he had his inoculations, and I had to drive the van, because they have completely knocked him out this time. By evening he had quite a fever and had to go to bed. Out of the question for him to scrub out the shed, or do anything. It will just have to wait until another day. Am acquiring a lovely tan as my normal dress is shorts and shirt, and it is much healthier-looking than the tan I collected in the tropics, which always left me looking like a yellow leaf.

The hay is about ready for leading, but we have no one to lead it, and must wait until Old Binks can find the time. Hope the weather doesn't spoil it.

Friday 23rd
Daddy has, more or less, recovered from his fever.

We have bought a cow. She was delivered in a large cattle wagon. A shorthorn, red and white, she is very, very beautiful, with big brown eyes and crisp curls between her uneven horns and, we are assured, a very placid nature. Believe it or not, she really has a short horn. I fell in love with her at first sight and christened her Clarabella. As the cowhouse was 'forbidden territory' until we were 'passed', we had to make her a temporary stall in the barn, where Daddy milked her. She gives a lot of milk, as she is newly calven; the white enamel pail was full of the foamy white liquid. What a shame that she has been parted from her baby so soon! She looks rather lost. The kittens were very appreciative of the fresh milk, but gluttons and soon their tiny tummies were bulging. As we had more than we needed, we gave some to the *Folies Bergères* and they fought over it, a rare treat indeed!

David has broken up for the summer holidays, so we went to Richmond to collect him. He came out clutching his case and a wooden coffee table he has been making for my birthday. I am very impressed, it is just what I want and, although my birthday isn't until December, we can make use of it now. By the time we got to Sutton Bank, the fog had come down like a thick blanket. I was glad I wasn't driving, as we had to feel our way slowly up. By the time we got home, the rain was pouring down and the polish on the table was spotted as David dashed into the house with it. What a disappointment, still, it's only a few spots. As David has a party on tomorrow, I suppose that means we shall have to take him to catch the train. That's the worst of these outlying places, but he'll have to find his own way back.

Saturday 24th
While we were away taking David to catch his train, Clarabella escaped out of the field we had put her in. Oh! these fences! I suppose she must have been feeling very lonely. After searching the lanes, we eventually found her across at Old Binks', contentedly grazing with his cows. As we were trying to

separate her from the herd, she, determined not to come back with us, jumped, or attempted to jump, a barbed wire fence, and in the process tore one of her teats. What a ghastly mess! It is a nasty jagged tear. Old Binks produced a halter and I dashed off to telephone the vet. Clarabella, quietened, slowly followed Daddy back, at the end of the halter, and soon was safely back in her own stall. The vet arrived, put a couple of stitches in, and all was as well as could be expected. Old Binks solved the problem of milking by offering to come over and do it for us until she is better. What a good sort he is! And so much more experienced than we are. We must now get the cowhouse finished and 'passed'. Clarabella needs a home. Wonder how long it will take for her to heal? Amazing people, vets, they take everything in their stride.

Sunday 25th
Sunday is a day of rest, but not for us. We must get this cowhouse finished, we really must! Then there is the feeding, watering and egg collecting, and egg washing, where necessary. We were in the midst of our scrubbing activity, the sun was shining, making it harder to work inside, when a car drove up and out stepped a man, his wife, a boy of about 12 and a small girl. We were very puzzled at their arrival until they explained that they had seen the advert in the paper and wondered if we would take Malcolm for a week. Malcolm had come to see if he would like it, and it seemed that he would. I had completely forgotten all about the advertisement, and shan't really have time to be bothered taking in children. Soon I shall have all the work to do, with only David and Vivienne to help. Still I can hardly refuse because I did put the advert in, so Malcolm is coming for the first week in August.

Morning and evening, at milking time, we have to go for Old Binks and take him back in the van. We have agreed to let him have so much of the milk as payment for his kindness. Clarabella is a bit touchy, but he certainly knows how to deal with her.

Monday 26th

Our first real market day. We had a crate of eggs, well not quite a full crate, but half full. We don't get paid for them until next week, when we get a form setting out the grade and price. At last we shall have a little money coming in, instead of it all going out. The packing station van parks near the clock in the Market Square, which is very handy for all concerned. All our shopping has to be done while we are in town.

Tuesday 27th

Vivienne's summer holidays start today and we have to collect her from Hunmanby. We have no trouble with luggage as we can easily put her trunk in the back of the van. It is quite comfortable for passengers now. Begging an old car seat from Mr Banks at the top, we fixed a piece of wood for the back of the seat to lean against. This is luxury so long as it doesn't slip, then all the passengers fall backwards. As the passengers are nearly always youngsters, this causes more fun than annoyance. Vivienne was all ready for us; most of the other girls had been collected, or gone off on the train, and she was impatient to get to her new home.

The nearer it comes to the date of Daddy's departure, the more depressed he gets, and it is infectious.

Vivienne is going to take over the hens and is planning to keep records in an old school exercise book. She really means to make a job of it. I am very glad she is taking an interest, it will be a great help to me. 'How now, brown cow!' she says, as we introduce her to Clarabella.

We have eaten one of the capons, but the other one runs around with the hens in the outside run. He is so comical I call him 'Clarence the Clueless Cockerel'. Really I can't help feeling sorry for him, as I have always been on the side of the 'underdog'! The hens treat him with a strange contempt and we watch his capers with interest. The hens, not satisfied with their lovely run, try to fly over to pastures new. The wire is very high and sometimes they are not successful and flutter back to earth squawking. Clarence struts to the wire, as much as to say, 'Come out of the way, I'll show you!' He flaps his wings frantically and gives a little jump. It is really pathetic. I weep for him, although at the same time I can't help laughing. His audience, more contemptuous than ever, continues to ignore him and, bulging with complexes, he slinks away behind the shed to hide. The mighty male!

Wednesday 28th
Great news! We are now attested. The Attestation Officer came this morning. She was very attractive, and she 'passed' us. Afterwards she regaled us with stories of her different jobs, as we had a cup of tea. It was all very pleasant but I must say we are relieved that, after the struggle to get the cowhouse finished, it is not in vain. I think we are expecting blows now, and getting ready to cringe. Clarabella can now go into her rightful place.

Peeping through the deep-litter shed door as Vivienne was collecting the eggs, I saw her holding her hand under a hen waiting to catch the egg – 'Absolutely new-laid, Madam!' She seems to have no fear of these hens and pushes her hand under their warm fluffy bodies to collect the golden eggs, regardless of their pecks. I don't like them pecking me.

Clarabella is getting on all right and will soon be having her stitches out. I asked the vet about the possibility of getting a puppy. In his travels he might hear of puppies for sale. We need a dog in this remote spot.

Daddy has to go to London on Friday, so as to fly off on Saturday. He is dashing round madly trying to get as much done as possible before he goes. He and David have wired in the four pig sties. We discovered when they had finished it that they had put the pig wire upside down. Still that can't be helped, we shall know better next time.

Friday 30th
The vet rang up and told us about a litter of puppies at the dairy farm on the left just going into Thirsk. The mother is an Old English Sheepdog, pedigree, but the father unknown, probably a Lurcher. They are £2 each and there are one or two left, mostly bitches. I thanked him very much and we set off for Thirsk, thankful for having something definite to do. All Daddy's packing is done. The puppies were

absolutely delightful, cuddly round black and white dumplings. So soft to the touch and so friendly. They are only five weeks old; we bought one and, Vivienne cuddling her in her lap, set off for home once more. Wodgie is her name, we couldn't call her podgy, although that is what she is. We were all feeling a bit low, and fastened on her to keep our spirits up.

Daddy left it until the last minute. He had arranged to catch the midnight train from York, and we all went to see him off. It was a terrible strain, and it was a relief when the train steamed slowly out of the station. As long as I live, I shall never forget that journey back. I had to drive, in the pitch dark, through the country lanes, not quite sure of the way, and I was feeling so weary. The trees by the side of the road loomed up like gaunt shadows, as I strove to keep my eyes open. David was wonderful. He kept up a stream of inconsequential chatter, which served to keep me awake, whilst Vivienne slept in the back of the van. Easingwold, Husthwaite, Coxwold at last, nearly home. Somehow I kept my foot steady on that accelerator, and there was no traffic at that time of morning, so we found ourselves in the lane. Then the 'rum' corner waiting for me, darkly mysterious. We were there, struggling in bottom gear, straining inside us to help the van. Only a few more yards and we were past the danger spot. A sigh of relief escaped our lips. Now for home! There it was Bracken Hill, the letters on the gate shining in the headlights. Home at last, with two kittens and a sleepy puppy to greet us. We tumbled into bed, weary, thankful to have made it. Thank God for a good bed!

We are home. We are on our own!

Saturday 31st
Daddy rang us up twice from London. He is flying today.

I have started building up my stock. I rang up the cattle dealer this morning and arranged to buy three calves to fatten. The calves arrived in a lorry, about lunchtime. We hadn't any straw, so the driver left us all the straw he had, and we put them in the loose box in the cowhouse. They are very lovely, standing on their stilt-like legs, very stiffly; they are only two days old. How they must miss their mothers! I feel very maternal. Two of them are almost the colour of Clarabella, but the other one is white and sort of streaky red. The tiniest one is fascinating. We call him Ferdinand (anything less like an imagined bull, I have never seen); he is beautiful, with soft brown eyes and long lashes. The middle-sized one is not so attractive or interesting and we call him Percival, and the biggest one, the streaky one, we have named Jonathan. He is much bigger than the other two, but narrower across the back. Now there is competition as to who should feed them. I relinquish the honour, as I have plenty to do elsewhere. Calves are rough little blighters, and if one isn't careful, they knock over the bucket and spill all the milk.

We have made Wodgie a bed of hay in a cardboard carton. She can't get into it without help, as she is so fat, but puts her front paws on the box and then we heave her back part over and she flops. The kittens love this box and, whenever it is empty, they settle down for a sleep. If Wodgie spots them, she waddles across to the box and has to be in, when she sits on the poor kittens, making it absolutely impossible for them to sleep. They accept defeat and jump out, whereupon Wodgie wants to be out too. Dog in a manger just isn't in it! She shares her milk with them, however, quite amicably. It is a lovely sight to see a small black and white puppy and a tortoiseshell and a ginger kitten, all drinking from the same saucer. Wodgie also has a habit of just dipping her mouth into the milk and dribbling all over the floor, from the long whiskers under her chin. This will have to be checked, it is so messy. David plays with her on the kitchen floor. He pushes her backwards and she skids on the polished floor, then rushes forward to the attack. So it goes on until one or the other tires. She is altogether delightful. Whatever did we do without her!

August

Sunday 1st
The calves are comfortable at last. We set off in the van this morning to look for straw. After posting the letters in Thirsk, we eventually managed to beg two bales from Mr Banks at the top farm. Must remember to order some straw as soon as possible.

Malcolm arrived in the afternoon, with his suitcase, looking very smart in his school blazer. After his parents had gone, I decided that he had better change his clothes and put away his good things until his parents returned for him. I can't be keeping my eye on him all the time. He is a very quiet boy; maybe he will open up when he gets used to us, but he is very thrilled with the calves. David and Vivienne were very sweet with him and let him feed Jonathan, Percival and Ferdy, just watching to see that they did not spill the milk.

Clarabella is almost better and will be having her stitches out this week. David is thrilled at the opportunity of driving the van down for Old Binks and taking him back, twice a day. I don't feel that this is breaking the law, only cracking it; after all, he is a very good driver, and it is not on the highway really. I remember when he was 11, he used to drive our old Jeep up and down the beach in Sarawak, at each and every available opportunity. He will be old enough to have his provisional licence in February.

Monday 2nd
August Bank Holiday Monday dawned, not bright and clear, but pouring with rain; so, complete with wellingtons and macs, we set off for market. I have never seen Thirsk so crowded. All the normal car parks were full. We delivered our crate of eggs and then left the van in the nearest car park and walked back to the market square. David had some rabbits to sell. He shoots rabbits for a hobby and for pocket money as well. I must say he is very generous, and shares this with Vivienne. Naturally she thinks he is the best brother in the world. Today, there were extra stalls in the market and cheapjacks and salesmen were volubly exalting their goods. This, fascinates me. The selling was fast and furious and the children had to drag me away, after I had bought some teatowels. I was mesmerised. Lunchtime came and so did the sun. It burned down from a cloudless blue sky on to steaming pavements. We were definitely overdressed! Vivienne and I went to have our hair cut and left the boys to their own devices. My hairdresser is very interested in our venture at Bracken Hill, and we spent a very pleasant half-hour. We finished our shopping and after lunch at our little café, set off

29

for home. Negotiating Sutton Bank safely, I thought my troubles were over as we jogged our way down the lane towards home, but it is fatal to even think such thoughts. Just as we came over the top of the bank leading to our gate, there was a tractor chugging its way slowly up towards us. Nothing for it but to back the van up the hill, a steep hill at that. I made it, and parked on the grass verge to wait until the tractor got past. It was Old Binks. 'Weel dun,' he said, praise indeed! When we finally got home, the deep litter hens were out. A bunch of them had leaned too heavily on the wire door, which had been insecurely fastened by person or persons unknown, and found their freedom. Who could blame them for wanting a little sunshine? It was comparatively easy getting them back in, with three helpers. I know the hens miss the fresh green grass, so I have invented a kind of wire sling, which hangs in the deep litter shed, and which Vivienne fills up, at regular intervals, with luscious green grass. This provides the hens with exercise and fun, I hope, jumping up for it.

The calves are developing bad habits by being together, so we are going to separate them. The loose box can easily be made into two by putting a rail across, and a rail across the spare cow stall will make another pen. I have arranged to have some straw from Old Binks, for the time being.

Tuesday 3rd
I think Malcolm is enjoying his holiday. I hope so; but he says nothing at all, and never voices an opinion to me. He must talk to David when they go out shooting, and he likes to go after the rabbits. Vivienne's appointment with the dentist in Scarborough. We had to get all the work done before we set off, but made a day of it. Uncle Cecil has been our dentist since the children were babies, so Vivienne is never nervous about visiting him. On our return, we called in at Ida's for tea, and Granny told us that Aunt Sarah had died at the age of 91. What an amazing woman she had been. I remember she used to terrify us when we were children, but I realised her worth when I grew older; her bark was always worse than her bite. She must be the last of Dad's family. Another link with the old world of childhood gone. Granny, as always, is interested in our doings, and we told her all about the antics of the *Folies*

30

Bergères, Wodgie, Kuning, Torty and Clarabella. She knows them all already. Art is a very good gardener, almost the best in Yorkshire, and we always come back laden with produce from the garden. Strawberries, cabbages and potatoes, a goodly haul! Wish our garden was in growing order, but it is just wilderness – as yet...

Wednesday 4th
Have fixed up the calves in their separate pens. It is now much easier to feed them. Jonathan is in the cow stall, as this is the biggest, and Ferdy and Percival are separated by a rail. Now they can't quarrel who has to feed first and try to put two heads into one bucket. Two into one won't go!

David let Malcolm have the gun by himself this morning. I didn't realise this, until I saw Malcolm coming a back with the gun under his arm and a rabbit in his hand. He was thrilled to bits, but what a shock for me. I have always had a horror of guns, and now here was my responsibility coming strolling across the field with one under his arm. How many accidents have happened through carelessness with guns, I wonder? I wasn't having any, if I could help it. I gingerly took the gun away from him and said he must never have it again without David's supervision, and put it away. I was quite sure it was loaded, but I daren't touch the thing. When David came in, I had a few strong words to say to him and, sure enough, when he looked at the gun, it was loaded. He made it safe, and I breathed again. Another escape.

Clarabella has had her stitches taken out. She is now our cow once more and David and I must share the milking.

Letter from Daddy from Geneva; he must have posted it en route.

Thursday 5th
The weather is very wet and dismal, and I am getting very worried about the hay. It is getting blacker and blacker every day. All our turning has been of no use. I can't do anything about it, so must try not to worry about it.

My turn to milk Clarabella. It is hard work, but I suppose we shall get used to it. My wrists ache with the motion. Clarabella is very sweet and patient. As I sit there on the milking stool with the white enamel pail between my knees, my head sinking into her soft body, I almost fall asleep. She turns her head and watches me with her soft brown eyes, chewing her cud all the while. My wrists get very tired, so I stop and rest a while, 'I'm sorry, Clarabella, do you mind waiting a little until I've had a short rest.' She looks sympathetic and keeps on chewing; a short pause and I continue the milking rhythm, eventually finishing with a pail of foamy milk, after one or two pauses for rest. Clarabella is a very placid, restful cow, and we all love her.

David has invited his current girlfriend to stay, so, tomorrow, Hazel is coming for a holiday.

Have seen some rabbit nets advertised by the RSPCA, for humanely catching rabbits. They make no charge for the loan of such nets, so I am thinking of borrowing two. Probably we can get rid of some of our pets in this way.

Friday 6th
The weather is still dismal, showers following the early morning fog. What weather for August! We took David down to Helmsley to catch a bus to Scarborough, where he had arranged to meet Hazel. She is coming on from Driffield, where she has been staying with her aunt. We met them later on, and returned in time for tea. Four children now to feed, all with healthy appetites.

Saturday 7th
Malcolm goes home tomorrow. We decided to give him a farewell lunch, so now Clarence had to be sacrificed. We much regretted this, but he has been eating more than he earns, so it was the only thing to do. I couldn't kill him; I can't kill anything. I delegated the task to David; after all he is the man of the family. Very reluctantly, he wrung Clarence's neck; we were all feeling sorry for the 'clueless' one. Hazel was helping with the plucking, when she paused with a handful of brown feathers in her hand, 'I don't think he's quite dead,' she remarked. 'He must be,' I said, but to make assurance doubly sure, David got the axe and chopped off his head. It was a gory business, but at least that solved the problem. Actually I think he was dead all the time, and it was

32

only 'nerves'. I took Clarence's body, starkly naked, and put it in the pantry to await the feast. Poor old Clarence!

Sunshine and showers and Sutton Show. Four children to entertain. What better than a visit to the show! Rushing round, we got everything done and everybody ready. The parking field looked muddy, and I didn't feel like getting stuck, so we left the van on the grass verge well off the road. Malcolm had a guess at the weight of a small saddleback pig, and was very disgusted when he didn't win the pig. I wonder what his mother would have thought if he had won it. Tea, magic word! We wandered over to a tent where tables were laid for tea, only to be turned away. That was for VIPs and we must queue up with the rank and file. After tea, we were settling down to watch the Gymkhana, at least I was, because I enjoy that sort of thing, when it started to rain. Vivienne, who is bored with such sports suggested the Pictures, and the others jumped at it. It was out of my hands. We repaired to the van, piled in and set off in the rain for *Girl Friday*. Later, picking up fish and chips for supper, we got back home to find Clarabella patiently waiting to be milked. David's turn this time, while we got the supper ready.

The rabbit nets have arrived. Altogether quite a day!

Sunday 8th

A fine day for Malcolm's departure. His parents arrived in the afternoon. We had partaken of Clarence for lunch, and he had made a very tasty meal, earning his keep at last and going out in a blaze of glory. We had quite a party at teatime, seven of us, in all. Malcolm, resplendent once more in his blazer, and clutching his rabbit, waved us goodbye and off he went. I suppose he enjoyed himself; I hope so.

I am sharing Vivienne's bedroom now that we have guests. She is passing through, I hope, the 'film-star' phase, and has decorated her bedroom by sticking pictures of her favourite stars all over the walls. Richard Todd smiles down from over the wash basin and Elizabeth Taylor, glamorous as always, gazes down with a sultry smile from near the ceiling. Mario Lanza, Burt Lancaster and many others in various poses, black and white and technicolour, brighten our existence and smile encouragement at the end of a hard day's work. Film stars work hard, they say! There are film magazines too, which I won't allow to be strewn around. Vivienne collects these and stores them in the attic, in a safe place, where no one can interfere with them – as if we would, neither David nor I have time to be bothered. We wouldn't, even if we had. Still, I suppose children must hoard and be secretive. I do wish Vivienne would take more exercise though. She is always sitting around writing, poetry or letters or something. Of course she does do the hens, but that isn't sufficient exercise for a healthy teenager, and I am constantly asking her to take more exercise. Maybe then, she would lose some of those adolescent spots which dot her intellectual brow.

Monday 9th
Only four rabbits for market, not much pocket money for two out of that! The weather is just awful, and I have given up the hay for lost. When we go past the field, I look the other way, as it hurts me to look at it. We tried to fix the rabbit net, after market. It's a tricky business. In theory it sounds fine, like so many other things. The drill is to fix the net in such a way that it lies on the ground in front of the burrows in the daytime, and then, late at night, at the tug of a rope, the net is brought up to its full height. All the rabbits which are out feeding get caught in the net as they try to return home. Then, of course, it is a simple matter to just kill them, one by one. Something always happens to our net. It either falls down, or the rabbits stay at home, the night we fix it. No rabbits as yet.

The hens are laying quite well now. Most of our eggs are grade 1. We don't take seconds, misshapen or cracked ones to market. These, we use at home. Double-yolked eggs are graded as seconds, why, I can never understand, as they are really two eggs in one. I suppose they are really too big for the egg racks. We have had quite a few double-yolkers, funny how it's the pullets who lay these. Poor souls, sometimes they strain themselves, and then they have to be killed. Hens are terrible creatures, cannibalistic, they peck at anything unusual. I don't like hens.

Tuesday 10th
It was David's turn to go to the dentist today. He has had a bad tooth troubling him for some time. I felt really sorry for

poor David sitting there, as the dentist had quite a time pulling it out, and I suffered with him. He wasn't feeling too good afterwards, so we tried to take his mind off it, by going to the Pictures. Reaching home we had to set to and do the milking. Vivienne milked for the first time, as David wasn't at all well. I dosed him with Aspros and sent him of to bed. Poor Vivienne, her wrists were aching by the time she had finished, and I stripped Clarabella, just to make sure we had got all the milk.

The rain drips in endless monotony from the spout just outside the kitchen window. It is a forlorn sound in the deep silence. What price the hay now!

Wednesday 11th
I have ordered five more weaners. I don't think the five we already have will be enough for breeding. They are from the same place but have a different mother. Uncle D is coming over by train to collect the van, bring the pigs, and then return once more by train. It is very kind of him; I can't really leave the children alone here. At least I make that an excuse; I don't really fancy driving all that way. He is coming on Saturday.

David is feeling much better now. Only a very sore gum reminds him of his visit to the dentist. This morning he came running down from the top field with the news that there is a great big hole in the rabbit net. 'It looks as though a fox has found a rabbit imprisoned in it, and just torn it out,' he explained. I feel very bad about this, and we decide to take the net down and not use it again. Luckily we have only used one so far. I sit down and write a most apologetic letter to the RSPCA offering to make it good, while David goes to collect the offending net.

I must be feeling a bit fed up – I chased the children out from under my feet and sent them off to pick wild raspberries which abound up the lane. It was very peaceful without them, but also very quiet. They do keep me alive. I think it did them good to get away from the house too. They returned with an excited tale of having seen a viper, and 6 lbs of lovely ripe rasps. This put me on the spot, good and proper, hoist with my own petard. I had to get down to making jam. David cleaned out a pig sty ready for the new gilts and Vivienne and Hazel shared the milking. Poor old Clarabella. What a test for her patience. She is a really remarkable cow and doesn't seem to mind who does the milking and how long it takes. I think she senses that we all love her and is willing to put up with almost anything. Hearing lots of giggling upstairs, I knew that something was going on, but didn't realise what, until David went up to his apple-pie bed. I turned a blind eye to the ensuing scuffle. David takes it all in good part and can give as good as he gets. What it is to be young! He tells me that he may be entered for the Yorkshire trials in swimming. I am thrilled at the thought, but pause to consider how he can possibly get in any swimming practice. What a champion he was when he was in the tropics! Of course he has won prizes since he came home, but he doesn't like the cold water in England and, as the school has no swimming pool of its own, he has not had as much practice as he needs. I have found out that there is an indoor swimming pool at Ripon. This is about the nearest, quite a way away, but we mustn't let a little thing like distance discourage us.

The kitchen chimney smokes a little, so David has moved the cowl off the old disused chimney and fixed it on the kitchen chimney pot. It looks very impressive as it revolves smoothly in the wind.

Thursday 12th
It has been fine today, for a change. I informed the children at breakfast that they were going swimming – there was a bus at 2 p.m. to Ripon from the village and one to return at 6.30. I took them down to catch the bus and returned to get on with some work. As I came up the road towards the farm, I saw to my horror, that the deep litter hens were out. Now what! Only me to get them in. I have never had such a horrible frustrating chase, the beastly things kept going under the van, and, by the time I managed to get them all in, I was actually in tears, tears of rage and frustration. I hated those hens. To forget it, I set about making some gooseberry jam. Amongst the nettles at the back we have a fine gooseberry bush, and this year's crop has been very good. We have gathered the luscious berries, ignoring the nettle stings and prickles from the bushes, and they were waiting in the pantry for use. I made 10 lbs of jam and some gooseberry tarts and then set off to meet the 6.30

bus. The children were in great spirits, and their towels were quite dry. The pool was closed for cleaning or something, so they had spent the afternoon at the Pictures. What a waste of good swimming time, I thought, but they had enjoyed it. Vivienne happened to ask Hazel how her foot was, and it all came out. Clarabella had accidentally stepped back on to Hazel's foot when they were milking, last night. Off with Hazel's shoes and socks, and there, the most beautiful bruise you ever saw. I examined it thoroughly, no bones broken, thank goodness, but it must be very tender. Poor Hazel! I gave them all a lecture on the necessity for telling me when anything happened, and we had tea. David insisted on trying the gooseberry jam and declared that he had never tasted any as good. My morale rose. The gooseberry tarts disappeared. I wonder, is it better to make everything so good that it disappears quickly, or not so good, that it lasts?

Friday 13th
I am not superstitious about Friday the thirteenth, so didn't worry about today. Vivienne and Hazel get on very well. Of course they are much the same age, as Hazel is 14, and they are both difficult to get out of bed in the morning. David uses the wet sponge method, which is very effective.

I cleared up a lot of rubbish from the shed at the back, and took it to the tip in the field, and I also emptied the dustbin. No dust cart up here; I make paths with the ashes and collect the tins, and everything the pigs won't eat, in the dustbin, and empty it at regular intervals. We have a very pretty tip, situated in a dip, with hawthorn bushes round it, hiding its rusty treasures in the folds of its greenery. I walked along the path to the tip, then, leaving the barrow, I continued along the path to the spring which supplies the water to the house. This is in a deep gulley which I call 'The Valley of Lost Horizons', because the first time I walked right along it, I could see nothing but the sky. This valley fascinates me, but the nettles are fantastically high there now, and we can't go far.

A favourite game of ours is Mahjong, so we have taught Hazel how to play. As I finally got down to writing my letters, I heard sounds of riotous laughter coming from the sitting room. Bracken Hill is coming into its own.

Regularly, a full account of all our doings wings its way across the world to Sarawak.

Saturday 14th
It was lovely this morning; the sun shone and everybody was happy. I got all done up and dusted, and left the children to it. As I got into the van to set off to meet Uncle D at York station, Vivienne said, 'Don't worry, Mummy, we'll have a lovely lunch waiting for you, when you get back. Rabbit pie. David is just going to get the rabbit.' What optimists, no doubt at all that they wouldn't get a rabbit. As we returned up the final rise to Bracken Hill, I spotted Vivienne feeding something to the pigs. She told me it was an unsuccessful batch of pastry but the pigs didn't turn a hair. The second pastry attempt was better. The cookery book said, 'Toss in salt, pepper and flour', so they had tossed it in, not realising until later it meant mix the flour, salt and pepper and then toss the rabbit in it. They had really enjoyed themselves. We had a hilarious lunch, which was remarkably good, and we ate every scrap, except the bones. Uncle D set off for Wales in the van after tea. David and Hazel disappeared to shoot rabbits. They returned with a couple of rabbits and Hazel with a bruised lip. David had insisted on her having a shot and the recoil of the gun had caught her in the mouth. Poor Hazel, she is having a time, but she takes it all as a matter of course, and even allowed David to teach her how to paunch a rabbit. What a girl! I can never bring myself to do that.

Tonight there is a lovely harvest moon. It has risen large and golden, over the hill, and now looks down at us from a clear sky, drenching all in a pale golden light. Bracken Hill has an unearthly beauty.

Sunday 15th
Uncle D returned with five small gilts, much smaller than the others had been at that age, one particularly, as it escaped through the wire. Could it run? It was like a hare with Uncle D chasing after it – we roared with laughter, such a large man after so small a pig! Eventually they were all safe in the sty, and Uncle D, recovering his breath, began to look around for

something to do. He decided that it was time the shed was put up. The shed used to be at the bottom of the hill, and was brought up in sections when we bought the place. It has been waiting until Old Binks has time to get around to erecting it. Nothing would do, but it must be started. 'You'll never get it finished before you have to go back home,' I argued. 'Never mind, it's doing no good rotting there.' I could say no more. Night fell on Uncle D and David still struggling to put up the shed. A hilarious time was being had by all, with me, holding a torch, so that they could make it safe, in case a gale blew up.

Monday 16th
The shed looks gaunt and lonely in the rain. Why must it always rain? After market, we took Uncle D to York to catch his train. I insisted on David getting in some practice at the swimming baths in York. He was very reluctant and had to be chivvied into it, although he quite enjoyed it when he got into the water. He isn't getting enough practice. Afterwards we visited the museum, a most interesting place, and we enjoyed looking round. On the way home Hazel taught David and Vivienne the words of Gilly-gilly, and we all sang at the top of our voices:

By a tiny stream – By a tiny stream,
Lived a boy and girl,
With a tiny dream,
And the dream came true, quite unexpectedly
In   Gilly-gilly-ossenfeffer-katsinella-bogan-by-the-sea   –
   eeeeee.

It was all very gay. Usually we sang as we rode around in the van. It is a very 'singy' sort of van. I managed the rum corner very well, but my heart is always in my mouth, when I have to tackle it. I do wish the weather would improve and I can't help thinking about the hay sometimes, even though I know it is of no use. Home again to the milking, David's turn, while I made tea. We have only been using the electricity to light us to bed. Tonight the fading glow disappeared altogether and we were left in the dark. I have bought in a stock of candles and we have to bring out the candlesticks, reminiscent of my childhood. The wavering light, casting distorted shadows on the wall, is eerie, as we walk down the hall and up the stairs.

Tuesday 17th
Ordinary household tasks must be performed whatever the weather, the family has to be fed. We are all rather fed up with the rain, so decided to drown our sorrows and go to the Pictures. I am afraid I am an escapist, it is nice to just sit and watch someone else's life on the screen, and forget the immediate problems. Some of the seats at Thirsk are in twos, very nice for courting couples. It was a good film and I escaped for three hours, coming back to more rain pouring down. I don't like driving up Sutton Bank; it is a long hill, one-in-four, one-in-five and one-in-six, with a very nasty corner about halfway up. Tonight it seemed to frown at us in the pouring rain, and I was glad when we got to the top. It is heavenly to be home. Home! what a magic word. I am tired.

The cloak of responsibility is beginning to weigh heavily upon my shoulders. Will they be strong enough to carry it, I wonder?

Wednesday 18th
It has been pouring with rain all day long. I just daren't think of that soggy black mass that is our first crop of hay, up at the top in the four acres. Old Binks came over and was very displeased at the sight of the skeleton shed. 'Ah was guyin' ti put it t'other way round,' he complained, 'Noo, Ah s'all et ti finish it off as it is.' I knew he wouldn't like it, but there it was, there was nothing I could do about it. I made him a cup of tea, and this was some consolation.

The time has come to think of breeding. I have decided, after much thought, to buy a young boar and bring him up, rather than borrow a strange boar at breeding time. Boars are notoriously fierce creatures and 'the devil you know is better than the devil you don't', I think. I am watching the adverts for a pedigree Welsh boar, about 12 weeks old or thereabouts. We have ten gilts now, all thriving, and they are certainly eating me out of house and home. 'Give them all they'll take,' says the book. They seem to take everything and come back for more. It must be the fresh clean air of Bracken Hill.

Thursday 19th
Where does all this rain come from?

David really must have some more swimming practice. Secretly I know that he cannot be entered for the trials, but I will not give up yet. We set off for Ripon in the van, singing on the way. I am an awful coward, and just can't face the cold water myself. The tropics has certainly spoilt me for swimming at home, but I am adamant that David must suffer. Hazel and Vivienne kept him company, but he spent most of the time shivering on the edge, talking to Hazel. From the warm comfort of my seat in the gallery, away from the splashes, I waved and shouted, 'Get in.' I don't think he heard me above all the noise of the children in the water, but, if he did, he took no notice. School holidays, and a pool full of screaming children. What encouragement is that for a Yorkshire trialist? It was quite impossible, I could see that. He had a dip, you could only call it that, and rushed away to clothe his shivering body. Vivienne was enjoying herself. She is a good swimmer, and just as good under the water as above. All I could see of her, half the time, was her feet sticking up out of the water. This frightens me somewhat, but she always appears when she gets out of breath, and I heave a sigh of relief. Feeling a little guilty at having forced David to do something he really hasn't enjoyed, I took the children out to a very expensive lunch before returning home (at least it saves my having to make a meal when we get back). The rain still pouring down, we sped home, the windscreen wipers flicking rhythmically, slowing and quickening in ratio to the accelerator pressure.

Friday 20th
Hazel returned to her aunt's at Driffield. I took her and David down to Helmsley to catch the bus. David was seeing her on to her Driffield bus at Scarborough. We were all rather subdued, no singing on this trip. Vivienne and I returned home to the chores, and went back for David at 8.30 in the evening. The weather had improved considerably, but David was rather depressed. He always has hated saying goodbye but I think Hazel enjoyed her visit so that is something.

Old Binks and his daughter Helen's boyfriend Roy, came

41

over and finished erecting the shed. There it stands, solidly black in the corner of the big field near the garden, facing south to the sun. We always refer to Roy as the boyfriend, I don't really know why.

Saturday 21st
David's results for GCEs came this morning, and we are so thrilled because he got eight subjects out of nine. He failed Maths. Now how on earth did he manage to fail that? It was always his strong subject. Still, he can take it again in the autumn term; I'm sure he'll get it then. 'What would you like?' I ask him, in a rash moment. 'Oh, a red setter puppy, please Mummy,' without hesitation comes his reply.

'You shall have one, if we can find one,' I promise gaily. How many red setter puppies do we ever see advertised? I haven't seen one yet! He is satisfied. His depression has lifted and he is his own sweet self once more.

We decided to get the field cleared up – all those old kennels are an eyesore. As we were doing this, bringing the sections of the kennels in the van and stacking them at the side of the house, just below the eggroom window, we were hailed from the top of the White Horse hill road. It was Hazel's mother and father. They were trying to find their way down to us, and had taken the wrong turning and come past the Gliding Club. It was really amazing how we could carry on a conversation at that distance quite easily. Every word was clear. We re-directed them and their car soon appeared down our road. It was a very good excuse to stop work, but we were sorry that Hazel had gone away to Driffield the day before. We had a cosy tea, exchanging news and views and enjoyed the respite. It is nice to entertain friends and have a change of conversation.

Sunday 22nd
Feeling that the children's religion was being sadly neglected, I decided to take them to Chapel. Owing to my strict Methodist upbringing, I have emerged with a childlike un-questioning faith in God and his goodness. No manner of argument can shake me, it is too deeply rooted. I assumed that Chapel would be in the evening, as in every other village

I have ever come across. 'We'll walk, it is a lovely evening and it will do you good,' I proclaimed, dragging the two unwilling ones down the lane and along the road to the village. It was almost deserted, only a farmer, getting his cows in for milking, drifted along the street. The Chapel also was deserted, the services being held in the afternoon. I suddenly remembered that Mrs B had our spare key, so, making the best of a bad job, we collected it and set off back. It always seems further when it is uphill. We wandered home, Vivienne developing a sore foot. We tried giving her a chair lift with our hands, but it was too uneven and she is rather heavy for me, so she limped on feeling very sorry for herself. By the time we got home, we were all feeling rather disgruntled.

Monday 23rd
Market Day once more; how the weeks fly by! I haven't a minute to spare, and the days aren't long enough. We got some rolls of pig wire for fencing the big field. David had 13 rabbits for sale and we literally had to hawk them round; how we hated it! Eventually he got 12s. for them. Myxamatosis has reared its ugly head. Our rabbits are free from it, as yet, but housewives have stopped buying rabbits. They don't fancy them any more. Bang goes David's pocket money. No point in bringing in rabbits if we can't get rid of them without all this bother. We all feel rather depressed over it.

Georgie has written to say she will come and stay with us. We are to collect her at York station on Wednesday.

Wednesday 25th
The weather is improving. It was fine when off we dashed to York to meet Georgie. Taking the rabbit nets along with us, we sent them off from the station, back to the RSPCA. That Society has been very decent about the whole thing, and didn't make a charge at all. Now that myxamatosis is coming, the rabbits will be exterminated anyway, if it ever reaches here. I suppose it will, but it is an awful disease.

Georgie, who seems to get better-looking every time I see her, had to have a look round everything and was suitably impressed. She insisted on having-a-go at milking Clarabella. What a lovely cow is our Clarabella; I often wonder what she thinks? The number of different milkers doesn't seem to trouble her at all. She just contemplates, and carries on chewing her cud.

Thursday 26th
I think the weather has really 'taken up', as we say here in Yorkshire. It is very nice having Georgie to talk to. Adult conversation is necessary to adults. We discuss old times in the tropics and laugh at old jokes. Just one more try at David's swimming practice. I know it is a lost cause, but Georgie can see Ripon, a lovely city, and it will be a day out. Am I kidding myself? I know perfectly well that David will have to scratch. I wonder how many Mums have hung on so desperately to an idea? I give it up right now. No more swimming. After we came back from Ripon and attended to the family, we went off to Thirsk to see *Genevieve* at the Pictures. We all enjoyed this so much, we were in fine spirits and sang all the way home.

We must get down to fencing the big field. The *Folies Bergères* are getting too big for their pen, and they have eaten off all their bracken.

Friday 27th
The weather is lovely – it is really smiling on Georgie and Bracken Hill looks at its best in the sunshine. The Glider hums overhead, and a buzz of conversation can be heard as the instructor instructs. We always get a cheery wave, and wave and shout back, as the Glider hovers over our heads. We have laid in a stock of stakes from the timber yard at Helmsley and, with the rolls of pig wire, staples and a hammer, have all the equipment necessary for fencing, our immediate project. We started. David is so precise and particular. It must be straight. I am a little impatient, as he takes his line and pegs it out, then hammers in the stakes in a beautifully straight line across the field, continuing the garden fence as far as the brook. He staples the wire, carefully putting it the right way up this time, while Georgie and I hold things and carry stakes down, and space them out evenly along the grass. It is a tiring job in the hot sunshine and David's legs and back slowly become a golden brown turning to red with exertion. How often this

summer has he been able to wear his shorts only? We have to make the best of it, while it lasts.

Vivienne, much to my amusement, decided that Wodgie wasn't getting enough exercise. She set off with the little thing up the road and disappeared over the top, a tall girl with a small black and white puppy at her heels. She returned about an hour later, carrying an exhausted bundle. Poor little Wodgie; all she wants to do now is sleep.

I have found my boar pig. There is an advertisement in the local paper. I must ring up and order one and then we can collect it on Monday. At least that will be one more step towards our goal.

Sunday 29th
The good weather has broken and it poured with rain this morning, slowly clearing towards evening. We went down to Helmsley to collect Tony, who is coming to stay with us for the night. David is wildly excited. He came running out of the house just before lunch, waving the local paper aloft in triumph. 'Mummy, Mummy, there is an advertisement for the sale of red setter puppies at Yarm, and they are only £7 7s. each, pedigrees at that. May I ring up and see if there are any left?' I had to agree. There were some left, and David arranged to collect one on Monday. Yarm is some distance from Thirsk, but 'reachable'. It's funny but Wodgie seems to know. From the moment David got so excited, she became very fussy and needed lots of attention, much more so than usual. We all petted and fussed her extra-specially. The air of Bracken Hill is electric with expectation.

Monday 30th
What a day! It was a lovely morning, bright and shining. As we had lots to do, we all got up early and set off for Thirsk first, dropping the crate of eggs (not literally) at the packing station van very early, surprising the men in charge. We had given Wodgie an extra petting before we left. She is so cuddly, this is no hardship. Georgie sat in the seat beside me and the three very large children sat at the back. We found our way to Yarm quite easily and did some shopping there, as we were searching for the address. We found it at last, a joiner and

45

undertaker's shop, and the puppies were in an upstairs room in the shed. They were delightful. The bitch has had 12 puppies in her litter and the breeder is selling them cheaply to get rid of them as the remaining ones are already three months old, and are eating him out of house and home. We had a debate as to which one to have, they were all so lovely. The owner advised a dog, as we have already got a bitch; he said another bitch might fight with Wodgie. With my head telling me I was adding yet one more problem to my already overloaded stack, I listened to my heart, and fell completely and absolutely for one of the dog puppies, which would insist on giving us his paw. He is a lovely colour and has a tiny white spot on his chest. The cheque changed hands, and David had his dog. He was deliriously happy, grinning all over his face. We set off back to the van, David clutching a writhing ecstatic red setter puppy. It was almost lunchtime, so we decided to have lunch at The Black Bull. Putting the puppy in the van, we lunched quite happily. On our return, we found a very untidy van and a very bloated puppy. He had eaten a hole right through the middle of a loaf of bread, and had scattered several of the other parcels. What a mess! Somehow, in the excitement, I hadn't thought; I should have known better. Still! We tidied up the parcels, packed ourselves in once more and set off for Thirsk, en route for Masham, to collect a pedigree Welsh boar pig. As soon as the van started off, the puppy was sick, and he was most unhappy the rest of the way home, which was a very long way. So was Vivienne. Poor VC, she can't bear smells in cars, and, being a 'chancy' traveller at any time, suffered almost as much as the puppy, even with both windows open. We finally found the farm at Masham, through the yard of the King's Head Hotel. Then began the serious business of choosing a likely boar. I have never chosen a boar pig, but there is a first time for everything. From the six or seven weaners in the sty, I pointed out a likely one, and the farmer picked him up. He looked promising.

The farmer turned him over and I counted his teats, very professionally, he would do. We then put him in a sack and he was lifted into the back of the van, behind the seat. Vivienne was now feeling a little better, as she had had a stroll round, along with the puppy. We cleaned out the van as best we could with some straw, I gave the farmer a cheque, and we set off for home. What a load! A squealing piglet, with Tony silencing him with a sharp rap when he squealed too loudly, a sick puppy in David's care, and five human beings. As we passed through Thirsk, I remembered I had to call at the station for a sack of pig meal. We were now complete. Up Sutton Bank chugged the van, with its precious cargo, without a hitch. Home again! Now was the time when I missed my servants. We had everything to do.

First of all, we introduced the pups. Wodgie was rather suspicious, but the red setter was so relieved to be on terra firma, I think he would have been friendly with a lion, and Wodgie was no lion. She was snooty for a few minutes, but soon they were chasing each other round the lawn. It was a lovely sight, and we were relieved, but it was quite obvious, from that moment, that Wodgie was 'the boss'.

The boar was quite a different matter. We were rather tired and wanted tea, so we risked putting him in with the second batch of gilts, as they were about his age. Old Binks had advised us against this practice, as he said they would fight, but we had to put him somewhere quickly, and we thought they were too small to do much harm. The gilts were most unfriendly and set about him, nipping him with their strong teeth and he was terrified. We brought him out and rubbed him all over with pig oil, to take away his scent, and then put him back. We had to have tea, but kept dashing out to see how he was getting on. They were ignoring him, but before we took Tony down to Helmsley to catch his bus, we were thrilled to see that they had accepted him, and there they were, all lying together in the straw, some one way, some another, just like a row of little sausages. We all heaved a sigh of relief. Mum had to clean out the van and disinfect it. Guests couldn't do it, Vivienne wasn't very well, and David was too busy with his new puppy. I must have driven over 100 miles today. I feel dead beat. Bed! How heavenly it sounds!

Tomorrow is another day.

Tuesday 31st
It has been very hot today. Early this morning, I was warned

to expect a call from Singapore about midday. David and Georgie got on with the fencing without me, and I did jobs around the yard until such time as the call came through. Who on earth could be ringing up from Singapore? Daddy is in Sarawak. The telephone rang at last. Dashing into the study, I picked up the receiver. 'Hallo, Coxwold 248.' It was Daddy. How unsatisfactory these long-distance calls always are!

'I can't hear you very well, how are you? Oh, we are fine How are you? I can't hear you, this is a very bad line. All our love, we do miss you, etc.' One short moment to span the continents, and it was lovely to hear his voice. I went out to tell everybody about it and the weather was so lovely, I took the camera. I must have a record of David and Georgie doing all the work.

After lunch, we took a little time off, to sit on the garden steps and enjoy the view and the sunshine. I feel we have deserved it. How lovely it is in the English sunshine, when the sun really shines. We basked lazily in it for about an hour, then, refreshed went back to the grind once more. We have now reached the brook with the wire and David nails it to the giant trees, thus saving stakes. It is delightfully shady under the trees but the combination of trees, evening and water, attracts hoards of gnats or mosquitoes. I have always been a target for these monsters and we are finally driven out. My head is still full of bumps where they have left their mark.

Vivienne has thought of a good name for the new puppy. 'Brutus' suits him as he looks so noble. His pedigree name, 'Golden Pride of Yarum', is far too long, and not very appropriate. Dalesfoot Prince IInd, the boar has settled down. We decide to keep to his pedigree name, leaving out IInd. It sounds good.

A hot bath and bed. I am so very tired, I find no difficulty in getting off to sleep.

September

Wednesday 1st
Georgie left us today. She saw no reason why we should go all the way to York when she can get a train at Thirsk, so we

took her down in the afternoon. We spent the morning cleaning out the deep litter shed. It just couldn't be put off any longer. Didn't someone once tell me deep litter didn't need cleaning out? They should have seen ours; it was pressed hard to the floor, a stinking mess. As it's no good just looking at it, Georgie, David and I filled the barrow, then David wheeled it on to the muck heap. In between barrow loads, we went out for a breath of fresh air. The hens were enjoying themselves contentedly scratching and clucking amongst the grass and nettles outside. Georgie was absolutely marvellous, she needn't have helped with this job, but she stuck it out, and eventually we finished it. Sweeping the floor with a stiff brush, we scattered fresh straw down, until we got hold of some more deep litter.

Hens, en masse, don't interest me greatly, except for being machines to turn out eggs, but there is one exception at Bracken Hill. Vivienne calls her 'Henrietta'; she is a golden-brown Rhode Island with a bright red comb crowning her beauty. Considering the deep litter nests beneath her dignity, she flies up on to the top of the engine shed and thence through a broken pane in the window at the top of the building, down – down – down – with a loud squawking, to the ground below. She wanders around a little while, picking daintily here and there, and then finds her way to the barn. She has made herself a nest in the most inaccessible place possible, behind the corn bin. Vivienne can reach the egg reasonably easily as she is tall, but I have to lie on my tummy across the bin and stretch to my fullest length to reach it. Needless to say, I leave the gathering to Vivienne. It's her job anyway. Having done her duty, Henrietta has a look round, a scratch here and there, and, when she is bored with her own company, waits patiently at the deep litter shed door, until some kind person picks her up and pops her in. She is quite a character, our Henrietta, and we recognise her by the piece of red embroidery cotton Vivienne has tied round her leg. Nothing disturbs Henrietta's routine, not even deep-litter cleaning. She went through her usual routine, this morning, coming in from outside to fly up and out and down and round. Does a hen have a brain?

Getting more deep litter proved to be quite a job. We went

round the timber yards, but drew a blank. In the end we filled our sacks with wood shavings at a factory which makes poultry sheds.

I have enjoyed having Georgie, but I wonder if it was much of a holiday for her. She was really one of the family and joined in everything. Probably need a rest when she gets home.

Thursday 2nd
Today has been very hot. The thistles are tall and thick in the big field, so David and I decided to cut some of them. It was a very hard job, but we made some impression and then set about finishing the fence. This job dragged itself out into evening, the mosquitoes singing down. Finishing at last, hot sticky and very, very tired, we staggered home, weary, worn, dirty and terribly bitten. Vivienne was waiting for us, fresh as a daisy, with supper ready and waiting to go on the table. What joy! Eggs, bacon and tomatoes, food fit for the gods. We fell to and we both agreed that we had never eaten such a supper. She had fed everything, gathered all the eggs, and even milked Clarabella, right out, almost falling asleep over her; she is so soft, silky and warm. How is it that I either love Vivienne very very much, or could cheerily grind her into the ground. It has always been the same ever since she was a toddler. There is no even keel with her. It's all or nothing, but we wouldn't be without her for anything.

Lovely, lovely hot water, enough for baths for all. Then bed.

Friday 3rd
Clarabella ran away. David saw her disappearing over the top of the hill in the direction of the gate. All very annoyed because we had been rushing around trying to get all done before we went to Helmsley to do the weekend shopping, we set off at a great pace to bring her back. She must have known we were on her trail, because, by the time we reached Old Binks' gate, she was disappearing into the bracken. Then she was engulfed and we could only see the tall fronds moving as she clumsily made her way through. We tried following her through the bracken, but couldn't see a thing, the tall fronds were over our heads, so we found a large rock and climbed on

it to try and trace her. She had disappeared completely. Frustrated and thoroughly cross, we went, down to the farmhouse and, sure enough, there she was, grazing calmly in the meadow with the other cows. 'Leave 'er 'ere for t'day; Ah'll fetch 'er back ti-neet,' Old Binks said, 'She's cumin' inti season.' We were only too pleased to leave her; I could almost see a smirk of satisfaction on Clarabella's bovine face, as we retraced our steps. On our way home we met a young man, connected with the building society, who was coming to measure up or something. I'm afraid I wasn't much interested in his affairs, I had things on my mind. I left him to David and dashed in and rang up the Artificial Insemination Office at York, arranging for Clarabella to be artificially inseminated the following morning. I shall see to it that she stays fastened up when we get her back, until the deed is done. Then she might settle down. I suppose she needs adult company; she doesn't seem content with the calves. They are small fry.

The building society chappie was on foot, so we gave him a lift down to the village to catch his bus, and then we went on to Thirsk to do the shopping there. It was nearer. I much prefer going to Helmsley as I don't have to face Sutton Bank on the way back, but the 'best laid schemes of mice and men'.

Old Binks brought Clarabella back at the end of a halter; she is unrepentant but lovable.

My family is growing up. Wodgie and Brutus are lovely. Sometimes we take them down the fields with us, but they nearly always have to be carried back, and Brutus is much heavier than Wodgie. Poor old man, he hasn't much hair on his tummy to protect him against the nettles, and he rolls over and over in agony when he gets stung. We have to try and avoid the nettles, but this is well-nigh impossible as the place is covered with them. Now that the calves go out into the field in the daytime, I have put them back together in one pen. This prevents Jonathan sucking Wodgie's ears. She used to sit in his pen and let him suck her ears. No matter how we chased her, she seemed to like this, and crept back time and time again. I don't think it will do her ears any good, sticky calf saliva, but I think we have solved the problem now.

Old Binks informs me that he is going to lead the hay

tomorrow, if it is fine. Hay! well the stuff that is up in the top field. Its nutritive value will be about nil, I should think, but I am grateful.

Saturday 4th
A great day! Clarabella has been artificially inseminated. This is much easier than having a great bull about the place, or taking her somewhere else. Another step forward.

The hay has been gathered in by Mr Banks, David and Old Binks, and we now have a haystack between the barn and the cowhouse. A small one, but still a haystack, and it makes Bracken Hill look more like a farm. David had to have his photograph taken near it, with his dogs and the gun. Quite the country gentleman! I had to make an extra-special lunch for the men. Mr Banks couldn't stay, but we entertained Old Binks, and he entertained us. He has promised to get me a baby badger if he can, for a pet. He says it has been known for a badger to suckle cows when they are lying down, so they aren't very popular with the farmer.

It has been a lovely day, with somebody else to do the really hard work. We went for a gentle stroll with the puppies and finally ended the day listening to 'Saturday Night Theatre'. We are real play fans, and try to listen to them whenever possible. What would we do without the BBC?

We are now turning our attention to the van. It is a dark green, the manufacturer's colour and it worries us. It needs painting. What colours? We have finally decided on a mushroom top half, a royal blue bottom half and a black stripe in the middle. That will be really something. Of course it can't all be done at once, as the paint must be dry when we want to use the van, but we have the paint and brushes ready.

Sunday 5th
It has been a fine day; we painted the mushroom part of the van early this morning so that it will be dry for market day. It looks very nice, but makes the bottom half look very dingy. We are raring to go now that we have started, but there are always other jobs to be done. I don't like doing unnecessary jobs on Sunday, but we have to take advantage of the nice weather.

Wednesday 8th

Another lovely day. This afternoon David backed out the van and parked it near the back door. I always let him back it out, ever since the first day I did it and broke off the driving mirror. These van mirrors seem to stick out a long way. The Ultra Twin was brought out and placed on the milking stool nearby and we listened to 'Wednesday Matinee' as we started to paint the bottom half of the van blue. It was a very exciting play. Suddenly, I noticed that the van wasn't quite the same colour at the back as it was at the side, and I realised that we had been so intent on the play we had forgotten to stir up the paint. To crown it all, just as it came to the climax the battery of the radio konked out, and there we were, three disgruntled listeners and a mottled van! David was furious and I had to restrain him from taking up the radio and dashing it against the wall. Was the mysterious doctor the fiancé who had disappeared? We shall never know! We hid the van in the garage out of sight and went on to do other jobs. We have enough paint for a second coat, thank goodness; and I hope it turns out better next time. We daren't go out in it as it is. We are making a run for more chickens and David hammered the chagrin out of his system by building the chicken shed. He was bashing in the nails when a rat ran over his foot. I hadn't realised we had rats in that part of the farm. We were searching for the rat hole amongst the nettles when we came across a nest containing 15 eggs. The rat must have missed those; I wonder which hen laid them? She must have been very crafty, as we have never seen her out. What a hope, if she wants to sit; the eggs aren't fertilised.

Thursday 9th

Very carefully we gave the van a second coat of blue paint, stirring at every dip and, finally, there it was, a beautiful uniform royal blue. I have to keep going to have a look at it to make quite sure it is really as beautiful as it appears. What a relief! Now we may venture forth proud of our handiwork.

The holidays are slipping away; David goes back on Monday, and Vivienne on Thursday. I shall miss them, and try not to think about it. All their clothes are ready and there are just a few odds and ends to get. What a lot of packing and unpacking I have done in the past few years!

David has been doing the milking most of the time lately as I shall soon have to do it all. He sings to Clarabella at the top of his powerful voice:

'Olé, he was a bandit, a bandit from Brazil.' We can hear him from the house and it becomes a shade monotonous as he only knows these few words. Clarabella loves it and I think she gives more milk as a result, or is it imagination? I remember when we stayed on a farm in Tasmania, they had a radio playing continuously in the milking parlour and they had very good results. Vivienne vows that she will send a card to 'Smash Hits' on Radio Luxembourg asking them to smash 'Olé'.

Friday 10th

A showery day. We went through to Scarborough to do our last-minute shopping for next term and arrange for Granny to come back with me when I take Vivienne to school next Thursday. I think Granny is getting quite excited about it, but Ida is rather anxious. They admire the van and think we have made a good job of it.

The new poultry run is finished and ready for its occupants. I have arranged to collect them tomorrow from Husthwaite. Black Leghorns crossed with Rhode Island Reds at point-of-lay – 40 more beaks to feed.

Saturday 11th

A lovely day. The telephone rang this morning. It was the policeman from the village 'Are you all right up there?' he asked, 'there is a lot of smoke coming from your way.'

'Oh, it must be the Forestry burning off at the top,' I assured him and rang off.

We put the *Folies Bergères* into the big field. They went quite wild with delight at first, chasing each other round and round, their curly tails springy with excitement, then settling down to explore. Surely they will have plenty to occupy them there, rooting it over.

After lunch we got all dressed up to match our very smart

van and set off for Husthwaite, Vivienne nursing the radio turning it this way and that to get the best reception, as we wove our way round the country lanes. Saturday Matinée this time. An exciting ghost story. Soon the children were lost in the realms of fantasy, but I had serious work to do. The pullets were very small and didn't look at point-of-lay to me, but they'll grow. The brigadier caught and crated 40 for me and I promised to return the crates. We set off for home, 40 BL x RIR pullets, 2 children, a radio and me. The White Horse stood out clearly in the sunshine as we came down from Coxwold, and we had a lovely view of it. To say that it is our nextdoor neighbour, we very rarely see it.

Hens are the silliest things imaginable. After changing into our working togs, we released the pullets into their new pen, whereupon they immediately flew over our wire enclosure in every direction. Talk about 'birds of the air' – it just wasn't in it. The air was full of flapping wings. Is it their BL blood? We had an awful time catching them, finishing up in the dark with a torch, searching the nettles. We just daren't leave them to the mercy of the fox. I suppose I could have put them straight into the hut and let them out the next day, but I am always afraid with hens, they are such silly things and huddle together in a corner. Some get trampled and some suffocate. I am still stinging from those nettles but I think we got all the hens in; David was counting. Vivienne made supper, bless her. I am very tired.

Sunday 12th
Another lovely day. We decided to return the crates and go to Chapel on the way back. David is feeling upset at the thought of going back to school and leaving me, but he knows he has to go. He starts studying for his Advanced Levels this term. I try to keep him occupied and take his mind off going. The congregation at Chapel was very small, the Chapel strange, but the Welburn voices 'swelled the strain'.

Brutus and Wodgie were eagerly awaiting our return. They demand a walk now, almost every day, and are inseparable. After tea we went for a stroll, trying to avoid the topic of school. It was a peaceful sunny Sunday evening. David is trying to train Brutus to 'heel'. Next Sunday, if I want to go for a walk, I shall have to go alone. Granny can't walk far, and the roads are rough. Heigh ho!

Monday 13th
We packed David's cases into the van along with the crate of eggs as we were going on from market to Richmond. He was very quiet. We set off as usual but by the time we had passed the hay field and reached our moorland, we noticed that all our heather had been burned off. What was all this about? My indignation was rising; then I saw one of the Forestry men cutting down one of my small trees. Stopping the van I jumped out, David following. 'What on earth are you doing on my land,' I shouted 'and who has burned off all my heather and knocked down part of my wall?'

The workman was staggered. 'That's your boundary,' he answered, pointing to a furrow which had been ploughed across the moor.

'That is *not* my boundary,' I stormed, 'that stone wall is. Will you please tell your boss to stop all this wanton destruction.' He was taken aback, but stopped his cutting and set off across the moor. I had no time to waste and we went on, surging with indignation, David more worried than ever, wondering if I could manage this. I was trembling still but told him not to worry. I shall just have to manage it. I'm afraid we left a very unsettled David at school, but he'll soon settle down to routine again and I'll write to him every week. When we came back down the lane, nobody was working on the moor and the equipment had been removed, only the charred blackened remains of my lovely heather were visible. As we were feeding up later on, a Land Rover drove into the yard and out stepped a very tall forestry officer. I asked him in quite politely, although my heart was beating rapidly. He produced his maps and pointed out that they had ploughed a furrow across the moor according to such maps. Being able to see the other fellow's point of view is a definite handicap. There it was on the map in yellow and green. I had to be firm with myself, and an extract from a 'piece' recited at some far-off Sunday School anniversary sprang into my mind – 'be cheerful and stick to your guns' – I stuck to my guns. 'I am sorry, but until it is proved to the contrary, my boundary is the stone wall, and you must keep off my land,' I insisted. He was furious, gathered up his maps and walked off, muttering to himself about silly women who interfered etc. I hadn't even offered him a cup of tea, but felt I needed one. I am a placid type normally, not in any way aggressive, and when I am roused it takes more out of me than the recipient of my wrath. Vivienne was full of admiration, 'Mummy, you were wonderful,' she applauded. Now all the correspondence will start. The deeds are with the building society and I don't want to be involved in anything that will cost a lot of money, but I am quite certain that the wall is our boundary.

To calm down we decided to go brambling and returned with a jar full. I can never resist a bramble, and brambling is such a soothing occupation. The dogs enjoyed it too; whatever should we do without them, they are such a joy, asking no questions, just loving us.

I have ordered coal and coke from the same firm who supplied the previous occupants, as I thought they would know the farm and there would be no difficulty. We are getting low and I must have plenty of fuel for Granny.

Clarabella shares the same field as the *Folies Bergères*, and we have devised an ingenious scheme for getting her through the gate at milking time, without letting the pigs out. Vivienne races down the garden and along the fence, rattling a few pig nuts in a tin and shouting 'Chak-chak-chak' at the top of her voice. The pigs, greedy as ever, race madly past Clarabella, who regards them with disdain, round to the food, I open the gate and our lady sedately walks through and straight to her stall, where, she knows, there will be dairy nuts waiting. I pick up the heavy chain and, passing my arms round her warm neck, fasten her up, taking good care always to keep out of the way of her horns. She is the gentlest creature. This plan of campaign always works. What shall I do without Vivienne?

I have given the *Folies Bergères* names now. Before very long they will be mothers. Number 77 is Jemima, 76 Daisy, 75 Topsy, 74 Buttercup and 73 Susannah. They are already acquiring personalities.

I have written a long letter to David assuring him that all is well.

57

Tuesday 14th
All the last-minute jobs and Vivienne's packing took up quite some time. I keep all the school cases and trunks in the little sitting room. It is comparatively easy to pack this way. I simply collect everything and dump it there and then we check the inventory and the clothes are in nobody's way. I had a call from the electricity company representative; he seems to think electricity may be coming our way soon. Do we want it? Do we!

Feeling a little 'end-of-holidayish' or 'beginning-of-termish', we decided to escape and went down to Thirsk to see *Happy Ever After*, which took us out of ourselves for a little while. Old Binks came over and when we told him about the Forestry, all he offered was, 'It'll dae yon 'eather moore good than 'arm, bonning it off!'

Wednesday 15th
We dashed down to Thirsk to have our hair cut. It looks much better now. How thankful I am that mine is naturally curly and the hairdresser always cuts it 'curly'. Bracken Hill air certainly seems to suit it, and I don't have to waste time having perms and things. The house has to be absolutely spotless for Granny's arrival. She is very particular and I just can't let her down. Housework has never been my forte but when it has to be done, I get on with it and I do like to see the house shining. I swept, dusted and polished industriously and the house responded. The stairs are still bare but clean. I'm afraid it's just one-of-those-things. I can't really afford staircarpet; it would cost as much as a boar pig. In the midst of all my activity there came a knock at the door. Who on earth could it be? I rushed to open it. Standing on the back door step was a florist behind a huge bunch of gladioli. I was thrilled to bits. They were from my husband for our eighteenth wedding anniversary, a bit early for the 26th, but very exciting nevertheless. I was considerably cheered, put the flowers in a tall vase in the hall and stood back to admire the effect. They just add the finishing touch. How sweet of him to remember! I shall have to be up extra early in the morning to get everything done before we set off for school.

Thursday 16th

Vivienne spent some time going round everything saying goodbye. I had to hurry her in the end. What a rush! I broke a cup in my hurry, and I'm glad it was I and not Vivienne. Everything seems to happen to her. At last we were off, and what a relief to be sitting down at last. Vivienne, in her smart blue costume, rattled on at my side, giving me instructions on how to look after the hens and keep the records. We finally arrived at school and she was immediately caught up in her other life. Where would she be this term, in a dorm or a room? She forgot her hat, coat and gloves. I discovered them on my way to collect Granny and had to return with them. What a girl!

Granny's case was packed and ready, and so was she. We had one of Ida's lovely Yorkshire teas and, with many injunctions to look after Granny, we set off for home. What a step for an old lady of 76 to take, although she never seems old to me, she is wonderful. Not very big, just comfortable, she has a very sweet pink face, silver curly hair, blue eyes and an outsize sense of fun. I must confess there are times when I have qualms, but she is very fit, only a twinge of rheumatism at times, and one or two corns. To me, there is no one in the world like her. I wonder how she will like her new home? She is going to do all the housework, except the very heavy work, shaking rugs etc, and what a relief that is to me. I know perfectly well that she'll do it much better than I can ever do. There will be quite enough to occupy me outside. Arriving home she went on a tour of inspection, missing nothing. 'I don't like that brick fireplace,' she said, as soon as she saw the rough brick fireplace in the sitting room. 'But they are the latest,' I excused. 'I don't care, I shall never like it, I shan't be able to do anything with it, it is so rough.' She soon found where everything was kept and set about making a cup of tea, putting on her clean pinny first, while I changed and went outside to feed the hens, gather the eggs, feed the pigs, milk the cow, feed the calves, feed the kittens and the puppies. It's all feeding. I now have ten gilts, one boar, one cow, three calves, nearly 200 hens, two dogs and two cats. Only the hens are bringing in any money. I just couldn't manage without the allowance Daddy makes me, and that nearly all goes in school fees even so, and the capital is dwindling. How does one balance the building up of the farm and the sinking of the capital? I have a little shelf in my mind where I put all my problems in neat little parcels 'To be thought of some other time' and get on with the immediate necessities.

I have been writing to the county council about the state of the lane leading to Bracken Hill. I noticed it today; it is worse than ever. The road men dig deep culverts across the road surface to let the water drain away. This may be a good idea to save the surface of the road, but it is not good for the van. Always, these culverts appear at the bottom of any dip or hill, and I can't get a run at the hill without the van lurching and upsetting my passengers. The one near the gate is a constant danger. I only filled it in the other day and now it is dug out again. I don't suppose I shall get anywhere with my letters but I can but try.

I have had a letter from the coal people saying they won't deliver my order, but will leave it at the bottom of Sutton Bank. I have visions of poor little me with the van bringing tons of coal and coke up from the bottom of Sutton Bank. Not me! I wrote immediately to the local coal officer complaining. He has been very sweet about the whole thing and has given me permission to collect a sack of coal in Thirsk, for our immediate needs, until he gets the thing straightened out. What a lot of letters I have to write. Will anything ever go right?

Granny and I are sharing Vivienne's room, and it is beautifully warm at bedtime; all the afternoon sunshine has been flooding in. We went to bed early as we were both tired and were just dropping off to sleep when there was the sound of an aeroplane flying very low whizzing past the house at terrific speed, then crash and an explosion. It was very frightening. I looked out of the window but could see nothing. Silence engulfed us once more. What can it have been?

What a start!

Friday 17th

A very windy day. Feeling very sorry for the calves, who are still only babies, I hit on the idea of providing them with a windshield. It looks a bit Heath-Robinsonish but at least it serves its purpose.

The south-east wind is my enemy. It sweeps up from the valley, breathes under the back door, draws up the Aga to red fury, then black despair and finally death, the water bubbling ferociously in the cylinder. There isn't a thing I can do about it. Lighting the Aga is a major operation. It has to be dismantled completely underneath, thoroughly cleaned out and should be lighted with charcoal. I find it easier to use live coke from the kitchen fire, but this means banking up the fire and waiting for it to get red hot and then there is the awful smell of sulphur. My eyes smart. Sometimes it works, sometimes it doesn't. I hate the Aga going out, as of course the water gets cold too.

Saturday 18th
Glorious weather seems to smile on Granny.

The pigs got out; why should they want to get out of that lovely big field? They jump over into the garden and I don't want them in there, even though it is rather a wilderness. I am trying to rescue the two lawns. These pigs are a nuisance and waste my time in getting them back in. Clarabella is in the other field now that Vivienne has gone back to school. I was fixing the fence with bits of wire and old doors etc, when I stepped back on to a nail which was sticking out of a plank of wood. It went right through my wellington and into my foot. I was suddenly struck by an awful thought. What if something should happen to me? Nothing must happen to me! I rushed to the bathroom, soaked my foot and applied TCP. I shall never again leave a piece of wood lying about with a nail sticking up out of it.

Old Binks came over and met Granny. They found they had quite a lot to talk about. He had been at Ganton Wold and so had she, many, many years ago. 'It's aboot tahme you 'ad them dogs used ti t'cheean; they owt ti 'ev collars on bi noo,' he remarked in the general course of conversation. It was just one of those things which has never occurred to me. We made him a cup of tea; the Aga is going again. He told us a young airman crashed his plane on Thursday night on Hood Bank. He was blown to pieces. That must have been what we heard.

My foot seems all right. I dose it again to make sure.

Sunday 19th

Another lovely day; we are having an Indian summer, and we are really enjoying it. I am glad the house faces south, it gets all the sun. With its long sloping roof, it looks rather odd from the side and positively 'seven-dwarfish' from the top of the bank. The pigs keep getting out, but that is just one of those things on a day like this. I keep on trying to keep them in.

Sunday being a day of rest, I went for a stroll with Wodgie and Brutus. 'Far from the madding crowd', near the gate in my grass field, sat a group of picnickers. As I passed by they looked at me as though I were the trespasser and not they. Saying nothing, but feeling very tempted to remind them to leave no litter, I walked on. I am not a spoilsport, and, after all, the best things in life are free, fresh air, sunshine and my lovely view. I could see York Minster from the gate, it was so clear. On my return, it was getting rather chilly, the picnic ground was deserted by humans but covered with ice-cream cartons, old tins and toffee papers. I cleared it up, reflecting that 'only man is vile'.

The leaves and the bracken are slowly changing colour and Bracken Hill is donning its autumn suit. We shall have all the beauty and none of the nuisance of the leaves. The trees are at a distance. I tried bracken for bedding, but it takes too much collecting. Another bright idea gone west! I must order some straw.

We collected our very first egg from the black hens; they weren't very 'point-of-lay' were they?

Monday 20th

Granny's very first market day!

Getting up about 7.30 a.m., I milk and feed and water all the animals whilst Granny makes the breakfast and writes out the shopping list. After breakfast, I back the van carefully out of the garage and right up to the back door, then struggle through from the egg room with the crate of eggs, heave it into the back of the van and shut the van doors. I miss David's strength for jobs like this. Then, putting the milking stool near the passenger door, I help Granny in, put the stool in the van behind my seat, fasten the dogs in the cowhouse, lock the door and off we go. Parking is quite a problem, but, if we are reasonably early, we can always find a suitable place. Out comes the stool and a reverse process takes place. The stool must now be considered part of the van equipment. Granny is thrilled with Thirsk and market day, and I have persuaded her to go gay and have her hair done at the hairdresser's. Feeling reckless, we each bought a dress; mine is grey with a large white collar, Granny's maroon. I also bought a Tilley lamp to encourage my deep-litter hens when the dark nights come. Granny insisted on buying the collars and chains for the dogs. We returned home, up Sutton Bank, after lunching at our little café, and she didn't turn a hair at the steepness of that forbidding hill. In fact she seemed to enjoy it, interested, as ever, in everything.

When we got back, the pigs were out. The attraction of the garden had proved too much for them once more. It must be forbidden ground that attracts them, I think. They are very friendly pigs, and with a few pig nuts I can soon get them in again, although there is usually one left squealing, thinking it is missing something and trying unsuccessfully to push through the hedge. They never think of jumping back the way they got out.

The dogs are always wildly excited when we return. We got out their collars and I put them on. They just couldn't understand it at all, poor little souls, and when I attached them to a chain and fastened them, just out of reach of each other, to the garden fence, they just sat and howled. Seeing this didn't produce the desired result, they were quiet, but continued to look unhappy and pulled and pulled. We now fasten them up in the scullery at night. Granny is very proud of her kitchen and they are not allowed in, with their dirty paws. They sit on the mat and look pathetic, but Granny is adamant, and keeps a strap on the arm of her chair. Bruty knows that she only swishes it and he pretends to come into the kitchen, edging his way behind her chair, his eyes brimming with mischief.

AUTUMN

September

Tuesday 21st

Another lovely day. We did the washing and it was beautifully dry. I have learned to read Jemima and Co's minds, and if I am there I can tell when they are going to jump over the fence. I tear madly down the garden, shouting at them and waving my hands wildly. They turn away, like naughty children, pretending they haven't been thinking of it at all. As soon as my back is turned, they are out again. My attempts at fencing are pitifully inadequate. I am beginning to get a fencing complex.

Mr S came down from the Gliding Club and tried to sell me a tractor. Nothing doing. I can manage quite well without one, and anyway I can't afford one. He is an interesting man to talk to, and we spent a pleasant half-hour.

Old Binks came over later for a gossip. He has promised to castrate the calves when necessary, and to stamp my herd number, when I get it, on their ears. It is some time since I joined the NPBA, and now I am in possession of an alarming pedigree book, with columns for everything. I know I shall never be able to keep it up to date. Vivienne's records are going to pot; and my bookkeeping! I have always been hopeless at bookkeeping. Never could do it at school in my commercial course. But I do try; then there is the Min. of Ag and Fish Returns. The paperwork for my small family is unbelievable. I am always writing something, and thank my lucky stars I have my typewriter. At least my official letters look official.

My favourite Lotus driving shoes have been chewed by Wodgie, aided and abetted by Brutus. Unthinkingly I must have left them within reach of those sharp teeth and now they have no toes. I know I shall never get another pair like them. Daddy thinks I am talking nonsense and says I am making excuses when I say that shoes affect my driving, but my feminine friends agree with me, and I am certain this is so. Wodgie has started chewing the table too. The support between the legs is almost through; I have had to put some tin round it. That'll larn her! Brutus is fastened to the back door knob, so we have to lock the door otherwise he pulls it open, as it has a silly ball-fastener which is rather worn. I still love them in spite of everything.

Granny has started clearing the nettles which grow all round the yard. It looks better already; she does a little every day after tea. I must make sure she doesn't tire herself, and I watch her carefully, but she seems to be thriving on it. I know that she has her eye on the garden and that will have to wait. In my spare moments I have cleared the weeds out of the beds in front of the bay windows. There are remnants of lilies-of-the-valley there. I wish they had flowered, I do so love the scent. How peaceful it is here in the evening. Not a sound. We have very few birds round the house, as most of them stay near the trees. Nights are drawing in, and now we must draw the curtains. I am afraid that I have never bothered to draw the kitchen curtains, but now Granny insists. She doesn't like the dark night looking in at the window. I have had to altar all the curtains by hand, as the sewing machine is broken and nobody has had time to repair it. What a grind! Needlework has never been my strong point, and I have had a thing about it ever since I was not allowed to take it for School Certificate and made to take Art instead. I must say it looks more cosy with the curtains drawn. The gas light is not awfully strong, but we can read by it.

Wednesday 22nd
The Indian summer continues. I am very tanned and feel very fit. Work never killed anyone, my father used to say; I suppose not.

Coming out of the cowhouse this morning with my pail of milk in one hand and the stool in the other, I was halted once more by the beauty of this place. I just had to 'stand and stare'. The rising sun was shining on the windows of a train slowly winding its way across the Vale of Mowbray and it looked like a giant golden caterpillar weaving its path across the plain. The scene was breathtakingly beautiful.

There was a telephone call for me after breakfast. Granny won't touch the telephone, and comes running out for me when the bell rings. The straw is coming tomorrow, thank goodness for that. I really need it and this load should last me all winter.

In the afternoon I had a walk up to the moorland. I see the Forestry have given up hope of planting my bit, for the time being at any rate. They have put a wire fence about a yard my side of the boundary wall. I am raising no objection to this. What's a yard anyway? Goodness knows when this matter will be settled, but so far, so good. I suppose they have put the wire this side so that the rabbits can't jump up on the wall and then over to the tiny trees. Rabbits are really a pest, and there are still quite a few about. We have some lovely trees in the Valley of Lost Horizons. There is one particular larch; it is tall and very beautiful.

The pigs still keep on getting out and I keep on putting them back in. There's no end to it. I can see I shall have to put some more pig wire along that hedge. How I hate fencing!

Thursday 23rd

Granny has been here a week. How time flies! She seems to have settled down wonderfully, and is the boss in her own house once more. I have been wondering about the coal and now it has come. Five men in a huge lorry, with my full order of coal and coke, turned up this morning. What a relief! Winter supplies are now assured. The summer is over I think and today was very cold. We made ham sandwiches and cups of tea in gratitude and the men departed, one of them remarking 'rather you than me, up here.' Cheering, I must say!

The straw came a little while later. I was glad the lorries didn't meet on the road, otherwise one of them would have had to reverse. Luckily there were two men with the straw and they built me a tidy stack. I can't even lift a bale of straw so I couldn't have stacked it. My half-grown chickens were also delivered today. Now we have enough hens for me to manage.

Friday 24th
Market Day at Helmsley. We go down to do our weekend shopping there because Granny loves markets. Parking is no problem. A very big square accommodates the stalls, and the shops are handy. Old Binks, our advisor-in-chief has recommended a sack of Kositos to satisfy my hungry dogs, so we get one. I have never seen Kositos before; it is like corn flakes, and the dogs seem to enjoy it. I suppose it is filling; of course they get bones and meat as well, but my butcher in Helmsley is not as generous as the one in Thirsk. He saves me all sorts of titbits. After a peaceful lunch we return leisurely home. Coming down the road towards the farm we look across into the field. Jemima and Co are out again. It isn't quite so bad if they are just out, but this time one of them has found its way into the others and they have been fighting. It is Topsy and she is terrified as the others have been chasing her around nipping her and she is bleeding. I race round and round the pen trying to make her go out the way she got in, but no, no animal I have ever met will do this, and I am almost exhausted when I decide to lift up the wire, and she gratefully dashes away to her own field. I then have to hammer the wire back in place to prevent the others getting out. What a life! but there is no time to be bored.

Saturday 25th
A lovely day but I am a little worried. I was milking Clarabella, as usual, tonight, when she just collapsed on me. The bucket went flying, spilling all the milk, but luckily when I was knocked off the stool and fell against the stall, I only grazed my thumb slightly. Very concerned about her I helped her up on to her feet and ran in to tell Granny, saying that I would just nip over an see Old Binks about it. He is a great comfort. He just mixed her a dose of something in a bottle and returned with me. Standing on a bale of straw, he held her head back and pushed the bottle into her mouth, forcing her to swallow the contents. It was absolutely masterly and I was lost in admiration, and full of gratitude. He also finished the

milking for me as I was still feeling a bit shaken and said she must have caught a chill; she must now spend her nights inside. I do hope she will be all right; she doesn't look her usual self at all.

The grocer has decided that, as his old delivery van has now given up the ghost, he cannot deliver any more, and is leaving my order at the Hambleton Hotel. The order doesn't compensate for the wear and tear of the van down our road; I can't say that I blame him. I call at the Hambleton Hotel for the groceries but have decided that I might as well do my shopping when I am at market and save having to come out specially.

To make my day complete, the Aga has gone out. There is a north wind and it blows off the top of the bank and down the chimney, making the Aga sluggish, with a down draught, and filling the kitchen with gusts of smoke at regular intervals. I manage to get the Aga going again; we light a fire in the sitting room and adjourn to comfort and listen in to Saturday Night Theatre.

Ida and Art are spending their holidays at Dalton with a farmer relation and they are coming up to see us tomorrow. I do hope it will be a fine day.

Sunday 26th
Our wedding anniversary and a very dull day. It would be, wouldn't it? Just when I want to show off. Clarabella is still in and looking very sorry for herself just when I wanted her to look her best. Nobody will believe me when I say how glossy and sleek she was. Expert eyes will be cast upon her and I am definitely on the defensive already. The afternoon crept on; I changed out of my working togs into my new dress, looking very glamorous. Soon I would have to change back to do the milking. Our guests came at last, walking over the rise. They hadn't dared to bring the car up, and had found it a long drag up the hill. I commiserated with them and showed them round. Granny entertained them while I fed up and milked and then we all had tea. It is very cheering to have company. The local farmers don't think very much of Bracken Hill as a farm. After all, you can't live on a view. Art and his friend weren't very impressed with Clarabella I could see, but

otherwise I had a good 'look-on'. I still think there is no cow like my Clarabella. As we were having tea, who should appear but Jack, another of my brothers, and his wife and two of his four daughters. It never rains but it pours. We always seem to have all our company at the same time. The sun wasn't shining and I couldn't show off the view, but Jack is very envious of the house, although not the isolated position of it. It is very quiet now that they have all gone. I took Ida, Art and the others down in the van and saved them a walk.

Monday 27th
Market Day once more and Granny's appointment with the hairdresser. What fun! In all her 76 years she has never had her hair done professionally. Now, a shampoo and set. The shampoo part was all right but when it came to the drier, she didn't like it at all. I don't like driers either. She had only been in a short time, when she shouted at the top of her voice, 'When are they going to take me out of this thing?' As she was being finished off, we told her that she could almost be heard in the street. The result was lovely, her silky silver hair fell in beautiful waves, but that is the last time I shall ever get Granny into a hairdresser's except for a trim, I can see. We met Ida in the market and told her the story. Granny's hairdo was duly admired, we finished our shopping, had lunch and went home.

When I have time, I like to take Brutus and Wodgie for a walk, and I usually go into the woods. I am collecting quite a stock of wood now, as I always return with arms full of dead wood, which saws up into useful logs for winter. I don't think I shall ever get over my 'old-woman-of-the-woods-gathering-sticks' complex. It is so satisfying.

Tuesday 28th
The postman Mr Fox, is a very cheery man. He comes almost every day, as we have a lot of correspondence. Leaving his bicycle at the bottom, he walks up the footpath through the fields. It's about a mile, uphill all the way. Bicycles are really no good to us; it is much too hilly; we should be pushing them most of the time. The postman also takes any letters I want posting. The dogs love him and when they hear his cheery

whistle rush out to meet him barking madly. We always look forward to his visits as he is one of our links with civilisation.

I am finding the pigs are very trying, getting out all the time, and all my efforts seem fruitless. I don't think they mean any harm; they are just hurdlers and love their freedom. If they had all been of the same age, I think the best plan would have been to have let them all roam together and just fence in the house. Then, of course, they would have got into the house enclosure. Still they aren't, so I can't.

Kuning is a thief. Granny caught her on the table eating the meat, so we have to watch her. I have never seen Torty on the table; she is a very lovable kitten and such a pretty colour.

Milking time, does it conjure up a picture of a shiny milking parlour with rows of sleek cows pumping milk into innumerable churns? Not to me. To me, milking time is a tarred shed with a comfortable cow chewing contentedly, and a little tortoiseshell kitten sitting on the stall waiting for me to finish the milking. As soon as I get up from the stool, Torty jumps on my shoulder, I stroke Clarabella's curls, say thank you, and, with Torty still on my shoulder, set off for the house with the warm frothy milk in the pail. I really enjoy milking time; it is soothing. Wodgie, Brutus and Kuning are waiting for me on the doorstep. They have to have their share of the warm creamy milk after Granny has taken our share, and the rest goes to Jonathan, Percival and Ferdinand. These calves are becoming increasingly difficult to get in. A rattling bucket serves very well sometimes, but at others, one or other of them becomes interested in something else and with one in and the door shut, two are at large. How do I get the other two in without letting the one out? It is a strenuous business, a game of tip and run. They enjoy it but eventually tire and decide it is feeding time. Granny and I have a good laugh at their pranks. I think if I didn't laugh, I would cry.

Two of the hens have gone off their legs today, so I have rigged up an isolation hospital. I fear these two won't survive, but at least the others aren't pecking them and making their lives a misery. Next time Old Binks comes over, I'll ask him to have a look at them, and kill them if necessary. I can't face killing the poor things.

October

Friday 1st

I think I have, at last, fixed the pigs. On our return from Helmsley, they were still in the field. We shouted 'Hooray' as we came round the corner and counted one-two-three-four-five little pigs, but not so little now. I am crossing my fingers and touching wood, although I am not really superstitious.

Clarabella is now in the field with the brook. This saves watering, and the only trouble with having her there is that she has to pass the kitchen window, and, knowing her insatiable curiosity, I have visions of long and short horns crashing through the glass as she catches sight of another Clarabella. I hurry her past, hoping!

Saturday 2nd

Today I did too much. It is a warning. I haven't worried Granny, but she noticed that I was a little pale and quiet, and mothered me. It is such a comfort to have her here. I'm afraid I shall have to take things a bit easier, I can't afford to crack up. It was because I cleaned out the hen houses. This is a difficult job, as one of them is on stilts and I can't get inside it, but must just shovel out the dirt as best I can. Then I spread clean straw on the floorboards, after having dusted them and the perches with disinfectant powder, as a precaution against red mite. I have put off this cleaning for too long. I shall have to tackle it more often then it won't be so hard, but it is an easy job to put off. There are so many much nicer jobs waiting to be done. I felt quite sick. After tea I went up and had a lovely hot bath and I now feel much better. A hot bath is my cure for almost anything. Certainly it relieves me of many aches and pains. I relax in the huge bath, leaning back watching the steam wreathe its way round a flickering candle flame, dreaming of baths I have had in other places and games of golf and tennis in distant lands.

I shall have a very quiet day tomorrow. I must!

Thursday 7th

Mrs Binks came over to visit us this afternoon and brought

some of her Victoria plums. They are jolly good, although she says the crop isn't as good as it was last year. We discuss this and that over a cup of tea before she departs once more to feed her hens. She doesn't have to do the milking though.

I see the telephone men have cut the branches which were shorting the wires when it rained, at long last. It is unfortunate when I can't use the telephone on a rainy day; sometimes things happen on rainy days!

Daddy wants a photograph, so I have made an appointment, at Sarony in Scarborough, for Saturday. It is Vivienne's going-out weekend, so we can take her out at the same time.

Saturday 9th
It was showery and I got my hair slightly damp; just when I had to have my photograph taken. Oh, well, it couldn't be helped; if I wear a hat, it flattens my hair, so I decided to take the lesser of two evils. The proofs will come next week. I left Granny at Ida's and went to Hunmanby for Vivienne. We were so pleased to see each other again; I think she imagines I shall disappear, and just can't realise I am really home. She wanted to spend as much time as possible with me; in consequence we were late home. It was almost dark when we got back and there, looking very unhappy were five hungry little pigs wanting to get back into their field. Why did I buy hurdlers? I have to do the milking by the light of the Tilley lamp, Torty purring contentedly at my back. I love that little puss.

Granny is thriving with the reins of a household once more in her capable hands. I think she feels she is needed, and it has given her a new lease of life. She's quite right, she is needed. I couldn't do without her.

Sunday 10th
The weather is still lovely. We were just sitting down to Sunday dinner; Yorkshire puddings, the Yorkshire way, roast beef and two veg, and rice pudding, when I happened to look out of the kitchen window. In an orderly happy queue, five little pigs tripped daintily past. Going the wrong way I thought; usually they came from the other direction. Granny put my dinner in the oven and I went out, and the fun began. I

put them in and watched to see where it was this time. A new place, just beyond the garden. They all set off at a great pace for the same place again and followed each other over the fence, and came back once more looking as pleased as punch. What can one do with such pigs? I really don't know. I put them in; then we have a race to see who can get to the fence first. It is a vicious circle, and I tire before they do. After all, I am older. Brain over brawn, they say. I fix the fence and then put them back in and watch their puzzlement. Our performance is watched with great interest by a crowd on the White Horse hill. It must have been very amusing from that vantage point. I am beginning to suffer from what I call 'fencer's elbow'. It is very painful and at times I have difficulty in raising my cup to my lips. Of course the pigs don't know that, or I'm sure they would be much more considerate.

Wednesday 13th
I am ordering another boar, then we can interbreed with our two stocks, and I have to get a place ready. He will go into one of the four sties until I get a run made for him. There is a shed at the back which is full of junk, which will make him a sty eventually. I love bonfires, so spend an enjoyable afternoon clearing out the rubbish.

Granny has decided to get some wallflower plants and put them in the garden, so we are busy getting the ground prepared. It is lovely in the sunshine, but a nip is developing at dusk.

I can smell gas in the kitchen. There must be a leak somewhere and I have made a note to get the calor gas man out to see about it. The cylinder is in a box under the kitchen window and the pipe leads through from there. I think the leak must be in one of the joints and the smell is most unpleasant. I have a very highly developed sense of smell, probably through living in the East, and I must have this faulty pipe located and repaired.

Trying to train Wodgie to bring in the calves is absolutely hopeless. She just runs up to them and licks their faces when they bend to see what she wants. What a farm dog! Of course I really haven't any idea how to train her.

Saturday 16th
Sid rang up this morning from Northallerton where he is spending a few days. He, Minnie and little Elizabeth would like to pay us a flying visit, if I could pick them up in Thirsk. Granny was thrilled to think she was going to see her youngest grandchild, and I thought up a few jobs for Sid to do for me. I wish he could stay a day or two, I could just do with his skill and strength for a while. It was drizzly, not at all pleasant, and I couldn't show off the view. As a special favour I allowed Sid to drive the van. One of my patients in isolation had to be put out of her misery, so he did this for me and dug a hole in the nettles and buried her. Elizabeth has grown since I saw her last.

The calor gas man would choose today to come and fix the leak, wouldn't he? Still it's done now, thank goodness.

We were having a cup of tea when Elizabeth pointed at the window. Gazing in at us, with a soulful expression on her face, was Clarabella. I rushed out, coaxing her away in honeyed tones, expecting at any moment to hear a shattering of glass. She is very obedient and followed me to the cowhouse where I rewarded her with dairy nuts. Now I knew she was safe. Visitors are stimulating. Pity it couldn't have been for longer.

Sunday 17th
The fog has started coming down on us. Sometimes we are in the clouds and it is clear in the village, and sometimes we are in the sunshine and the village is shrouded in a hazy mist. I hate the fog. It deadens everything and there is nothing but silence, a silence which can be felt. The trees have lost their leaves, but I do like to see them, and now can't. This afternoon it cleared a little and Old Binks and Mr Banks came over to 'see if we were still alive'. We were very pleased to see them, needless to say. They had a look round and decided that it was 'aboot tahme that there boar was separated from them there gilts', so set about doing just that. He might get ideas and he isn't supposed to get ideas until he is licensed, at the age of six months. They easily rounded him up and put him in the stable. Now I shall have extra work, cleaning out, feeding and watering, but it is so necessary.

Brutus and Wodgie are growing. They each instinctively know what is in the other's mind. Giving each other a mere glance, off they go, tearing up the bank, taking the fence in their stride, black-and-white and red streaks. How I envy their energy! They make me feel quite tired, but I delight in their liveliness. Another of their favourite games is to chase the kittens, if they can get them on the run. Kuning and Torty are up to all these tricks and keep well out of the way. Funny though, they never chase them at feeding time. I suppose they are too interested in food. Brutus is very clever at opening the little gate too. I have been in the habit of putting a tin of pig nuts on the gate post near the deep-litter shed, while I feed the hens. 'Let your head save your legs,' Granny has always taught me, but now I shall have to find another place for the tin, as Brutus found it this afternoon and knocked it off, and I came out of the deep-litter shed to find him and Wodgie enjoying a feast of 'forbidden fruit'. Wodgie has an engaging way of taking hold of the bottom of my coat and going round and round with it, and then pulling me on, as though to say 'Come on, you belong to me'.

Monday 18th
This morning was wet. We got all ready, as usual, but when I went for the van, I found it had a flat tyre. Thinking I ought to have-a-bash, I searched high and low for the spare but just couldn't find it, and had to ring up the garage. Eventually the mechanic came up and changed the wheel and took the flat away to be mended. I was most intrigued to find that the spare is tucked away underneath the van, very cunning. I think I am relieved that I didn't have it to do, as I would never know whether the screws would be tight enough or whether the wheel would come off. It was too late for market, so we shall have to take twice as many eggs next week.

Tuesday 19th
It has been a lovely day. We had to get in the groceries so went down to Thirsk and called at the garage for the spare wheel on the way back. I am always most careful to keep the van filled up with petrol; just can't afford to run out in these

hills. Granny bought some wallflower plants as she is determined we shall have a show next spring. I hope we shall; I love wallflowers, and the scent of wallflowers after rain is something exiles dream about.

Old Binks and the boyfriend came over. They had decided it was time to castrate the calves, so I lighted the Tilley and Granny and I made a cup of tea while they performed the necessary operation. Another job done. I certainly can't have three young bulls on the place.

Wednesday 20th
A wire came over the telephone this morning; the boar pig I have ordered has been sent off and will be arriving at Thirsk station sometime today. What a good thing the telephone is in working order. It is a long way off the beaten track for the telegram boy; now a confirmatory one will come by post. I immediately rang up the station; the pig hadn't arrived, but they promised to ring me up when he did. He came on the 3.20 p.m. and we went down for him. Whenever I go out in the van, I always take Granny as she doesn't like being alone for long, and she enjoys the trips. Luckily there was a porter handy to carry the crate and put it in the van. Poor little pig, he was very nervous and we were certainly aware of his presence. All the way home, I was working out how to get him into his sty, which was all ready to receive him. I backed the van as near to the sty as possible, opened the sty door just wide enough for me to get my toe in to open it, not enough to encourage the inquisitive pigs to investigate, and returned to the van with a pair of pliers. Prying open the crate took up a few minutes; then, lifting out a screaming, kicking boar pig, I scrambled over the fence, prised open the door with my foot and deposited him in his straw. Poor little man, he was so relieved to be free again as he had been very cramped in his crate. I shall call him Simon, his pedigree name is unpronounceably Welsh. Simon he is, from now on.

Granny has planted the wallflowers and I have put some manure round them, but not too near as to burn them. No shortage of that commodity here. I have been thinking about making money. Nothing is earning its living here except the hens; I have been reading about mushroom growing and

76

think there might be something in it. I shall send away for the spawn and fertiliser and have a shot at it. Try anything once. I have now finished knitting the gloves which will go inside my working gloves. I am trying to keep my hands ladylike, but when I look at them, fear I am fighting a losing battle. One glove finger wears out first, and until I get it mended, I have one workworn finger. Occupational hazard, I suppose.

Saturday 23rd
The nights are drawing in and I notice the gas is going down; I shall have to take the cylinder in on Monday and change it for a full one. What a business this is. I have to heave the empty cylinder out of its box and get it into the van. At the shop the assistant lifts the full one into the van for me, but I have to deal with it when I get home. Somehow I manage to roll it along, then manhandle it into its box and fix the pipe on the top. How heavy they are! Or am I getting weaker? I used to think I was very strong, but I am beginning to wonder now. I seem to get very tired.

I am planning ahead for Simon. I want him out in the open as soon as possible, as this will save cleaning out his sty. I have enough cleaning out to do. Today I decided to make the back shed into a sty, so cleared it finally and completely, and then hammered corrugated iron sheets on to the side, making it waterproof. What a joiner! Very pleased with my handi-work, standing back in the nettles, I survey it with satisfac-tion. 'Something attempted, something done.' Granny is full of admiration and praise. 'It's a lovely sty; you have made a very good job of it,' she encourages me. This is very good for my morale. I know I can always rely on Granny to build it up. Will it be good enough for Simon? He is a dear little pig; we have grown very fond of each other. He seems so lonely; when I go in to feed him, there is an undulation of the straw and a little pink nose appears; a grunt of welcome and there is my little Simon. We have a scratch and a chat and I think we both look forward to this.

The Aga went out!

Tuesday 26th
Letter from David saying his half-term starts on Thursday

instead of Friday and may Frank come too? By all means, I like to encourage the children to have their friends to stay. He tells me he has passed his Maths exam; I thought he would. I must now reorganise my week to fit in though, as Vivienne is coming on Saturday. I have lots of plans which must be put into operation while I have two strong lads to do the hard work. I think if we put Dalesfoot Prince in the garden, he can root it up and then digging will be easier later. Simon's pen has to be made on the bank too. Luckily I have enough wire and stakes. The boys can get on with it. Then there is the fence in the top field; maybe they can try that too. Or am I expecting too much? It won't be much of a holiday; Frank's father is a farmer, so he'll understand.

The deep litter is trampled down again. I am at my wits' end to keep it fresh. Old Binks is having a threshing day tomorrow in his top field. He came over tonight and says I can have some chaff. That will keep me going for a while.

In my spare moments, I saw up logs for winter; my stock is growing. I like doing this, for, as the saw bites its way through the wood, dropping the fine dust to the ground, I can think of other things, and, if the logs are not too thick, I dispose of them in no time at all. Isn't it funny how the saw never goes straight through, but always at an angle; I can never start again at the other side of the wood and meet my slice squarely. Do I qualify for a desert island, I wonder idly?

Thursday 28th
Had to dash around and get all done before setting off for Richmond to collect the boys. It was quite dark by the time we got back and then the milking had to be done by the light of the Tilley lamp. I did it tonight as I am in good practice and Granny was there to get the tea ready. What a rock she is! It's lovely to have young voices rousing the echoes again. Tomorrow there are jobs to be done.

I am sorry I missed the vicar. What a long journey for nothing.

Friday 29th
Today has been very windy, gale force, I should say. We had to collect the chaff from Old Binks' top field, before it all

blew away. Frank drove the van but, as he suffers with asthma, he couldn't go near the chaff. David and I struggled with it, our ears, eyes and nostrils full of dust, in the teeth of that roaring gale. At last we had it safely sacked and in the van, and home we went. The boys are so full of energy, they make me feel tired. They have decided we must have electricity. Candles are all very well, but! They have been messing about with the engine and I heard it throbbing; a small stock of electricity must have been built up because there was a pale glow from the powerhouse. If the engine is run again tomorrow, we may have enough for the winter. We gaze in wonder at the faint glimmer which lights us to bed.

Saturday 30th
What a lovely day it has been for the end of October. Granny and I went to collect Vivienne, leaving David and Frank to make a pen for Simon. Dashing home in time for lunch, with two hungry boys to feed, we discovered the Aga was out. Need I say more! Simon's pen is now ready. David carried him, not screaming this time, he is a tame pig now, and we watched him glory in his freedom. He loves his cosy little nest at the back. Now we can watch him, as well as the hens, from the kitchen window. The bank is very steep, but the exercise will keep him fit. No more cleaning out of Simon when I have cleaned out his sty this once.

Who left the powerhouse light on? Nobody admits it, but there isn't a spark of electricity left in the batteries. Boys will be boys, I suppose, and sometimes mechanics, but this time the engine is solid and will not budge. I fear electricity is out!

Sunday 31st
Today was no day of rest; we have to use up all available time. David and Frank made a pen for Dalesfoot Prince in the garden. They carried straw bales into it and we built him a house of straw. I could imagine the wolf 'huffing and puffing' but I don't think he could have blown this house in. It faces south and gets all that sun. He is a lucky Dalesfoot Prince. Being too heavy to carry, with four of us to turn him, it was a

comparatively simple matter to put him into his pen. He thought it was great fun to be in the open air again; he won't be six months old until December, when he can be licensed. Everybody thought the pen an excellent idea, but we changed our minds after lunch. We came out to see that Jemima and Topsy had been overcome by curiosity and something else and had jumped over the fence into the new pen. We had an awful job chasing them out. I hadn't thought of this complication. Clearly they don't understand the rules – no shennaniking with an unlicensed boar! The boys have fixed the fence. Hope it holds for when I am alone again.

November

Monday 1st
Market Day first, hair cuts for all, then a dash back with Vivienne to school. What a long day; darkness had set in before we got back home, and the hens and pigs had gone to bed without food. The only thing we had to do was milk Clarabella. David has got into milking routine once more. I am going to miss these young people. Vivienne always takes over the hens and watering when she comes home. It is such a help. The proofs of my photograph which came by post this morning aren't too bad. I have ordered one big one for Daddy and smaller ones for the children. Photographs are expensive these days.

Tuesday 2nd
David and Frank spent the morning fixing the fence to the top field. Really, that hedge ought to be laid; it is all sprawly hawthorn trees, but it will have to wait, along with lots of other jobs. Frank has had experience with fences and they were getting on well, when a piece of hawthorn fell on David's upturned face and a thorn pierced his cheek. There is no thorn in now, but a blue mark where it has been. I don't think it will get any worse and have put TCP on it. What a good thing it wasn't his eye! I breathe again.

The boys have to return to school. I have enjoyed their short stay and they seem to have enjoyed themselves too, even with all the hard work. They take it in their stride. How is it that a hammer just goes up and falls down so easily when wielded by one of these stalwarts? I am filled with admiration.

We were happily jogging along to Richmond, enjoying the pleasant afternoon sunshine, not a cloud in the sky, when, suddenly, out of the blue, a flock of turkeys charged across the road right in front of the van. I slowed down and thought I had missed them all, but one flew right into my rear wheel and there it lay, fluttering on the side of the road. I had to stop; I just couldn't drive on. Going back, accompanied by the two boys, I found the turkey not quite dead but fluttering feebly. I told the old man, who was standing helplessly by, to put it out of its misery. He did so and carried it into a shed in the yard. A young woman then came on the scene and stormed at me. The boys were furious, but I felt so sorry that the turkey was dead I gave her £1. She was so rude, I regretted it almost as soon as I had done it. Just imagine letting turkeys out to cross a main road, on a corner too. It's just asking for trouble, and I needn't have stopped. It wasn't necessary to report it to the police, being only a turkey, but the boys said I should have the bird if I paid for it, but I was upset and left it at that. Even if the turkeys comprised her livelihood, there was no need for her to be so rude. She should have been thankful it was only one.

The sun seemed less bright.

Wednesday 3rd
Another lovely day; we did the washing and ironing, taking advantage of the weather.

The pigs have thought up another game – getting in with Dalesfoot Prince – I discovered the whole five of them, Jemima, Topsy, Buttercup, Daisy and Susannah having fun with him. How I got them out still leaving him in, I don't really know, but I was completely exhausted. Now I feel good for nothing but sleep; my head nods over my magazine. I have been trying to read *The Count of Monte Cristo* but the print is so small and I am so weary, I can't manage it. Now for a hot bath.

Thursday 4th
Last time Old Binks came over, I told him that I had bought

some Ketchum tags and a 'putter-onner' which is like a pair of pliers. Tonight he came over and I helped him to earmark the calves with my herd number Y 8233. Now they are fixed until they are nine months old and eligible for subsidy. Roll on the day.

Since the top field is, more or less, stock-proof, I have decided that Clarabella must go up into the 'fog' as it is called after hay (Goodness knows why? I don't).

Friday 5th
Disappointing – I had hoped to have a good view of the village fireworks, but we can't see a thing for the fog which has come down enveloping us in its chilly silence. Visibility nil. I shiver.

Sunday 7th
Spent all morning trying to show Clarabella a short cut up the bank to the 'fog'; she wasn't having any, so I had to take her round the long way. How is it that so many of my good ideas don't work? She is quite happy with all that nice green grass and her milk supply has improved.

Monday 8th
When we got back from market we counted five pigs in the big field, but when we got round into the yard, there were five pigs from the bracken, in the yard, looking rather guilty. Something will have to be done. They have no bracken left now and they have rooted up all the ground in their pen. Something definitely will have to be done.

Dalesfoot Prince is rather a problem too. When I come out to feed up in the morning, as soon as he hears the buckets rattle, he jumps over the fence and comes to meet me. If he would jump back, I wouldn't mind, but he won't. Now I creep stealthily out of the house and put the buckets down very gently and, bearing his tin of nuts, dash through the garden gate and beat him to it. This morning, I had to push him back over just as he was balancing on the fence. We have to laugh! Vicious boar pigs! Vivienne says that Angela's pigs never get out and Angela can't understand why ours do. 'Put some barbed wire on top of the fence,' Ange advises. Visions of gory piggy tummies flit through my mind and I decide against it. I must rear these animals. When I read of all the diseases they can get, I wonder. Foot and Mouth, Enteritis, Erysipelas, Swine Fever and many more; I have to shut my mind to it or I should worry about them. They seem fit enough.

At milking time I go up into the field and call 'CLARABELLA,' at the top of my voice. She usually replies with a 'Moo-oo' and looks over the top down at me. 'Come on down, dear Clarabella,' I implore, to no avail. She stays there and waits for me. I take the short cut and she comes when she sees me in the field. She is getting very temperamental now, and won't be driven. She follows me, like a dog, close at my heels. Not being a dog this is a little dangerous for me, and I take a little run now and then to get out of range of her horns, but she soon catches me up. I can't help laughing aloud – down the hill we come – 20 paces then hop, skip and jump – repeat. But she's my pet, what can I do? One word from me! On the days when she doesn't answer my call, I know that she is over at Old Binks' and that means a long walk. I always take the opportunity of having a word with Toby while I am over there, he is so lovely.

I never realised the value of fences until now. I feel that the signature tune on this farm is 'Don't fence me in'.

Tuesday 9th
The bracken pigs are starting to get into Simon's pen. He is much smaller than they are, and they have nipped him once or twice lately, drawing blood. Nothing must happen to my Simon! I chase madly up and down the steep bank getting them out. Now I have to fence Simon's pen against them. I have decided that they must be moved into another patch of bracken, even though the fronds have now fallen.

The mushroom spawn and fertiliser has arrived. When shall I find time to attend to it!

The hens are not laying so well, it must be the weather.

Saturday 13th
The bracken pigs have been getting out of hand. Today I put

them in the sty and shut the door on them. I don't want to keep them in for too long, it is too small, but the fence must be moved. I started this morning. Finding that I just couldn't take the staples out of the wire; they have been hammered too deeply into the stakes, I decided the only way I could do it was to move the whole thing, pulling out the stakes and then hammering them in once more. I know it is going to be hard work but it must be done. I have pulled up the fence and dragged it across to its new position, but now starts the hammering in. The ground is either spongily peaty, or rock. How on earth can I put all those stakes in? It's harder still with the wire still attached to them. I must do it. I must!

I am tired.

Sunday 14th
I can't rest until I have finished that awful fence. What have I started? What I have started, I must finish. The fog came down and I couldn't see the house. I was completely alone on the bank with my stakes, my hammer and the wire. Alone but not lonely. After all, loneliness is a state of mind. I know I have felt much lonelier in the Raffles Hotel in Singapore than ever I have at Bracken Hill, isolated as it is. I think I may finish the fence tomorrow, but it is heart-breaking. The hammer head keeps coming off, no matter how I try to fix it. I have hammered in wedges and nails and all sorts of junk and it still comes off. It rolls its ungainly way down the hill; I wearily climb over the fence and retrieve it, then look round for some hard surface on which to bang the handle – this has always worked with brushes and brooms – but not with my hammer. Two more strikes – really I only lift the heavy hammer and let it drop on the stake head, as I haven't enough force to strike – then once more away it goes, leering at me on its way. If there was a handy wall would I bang my head on it? No, I don't think I would; I am the dogged plodding type and on I go. Granny is very soothing and always has the meals ready, at least I don't have to cook. She is a tower of strength and I am cheered by the sight of her fresh pink cheeks and ready smile, as I wearily sit down, drinking my tea, holding the cup in my left hand; my fencer's elbow has caught up with me again. I must now go and luxuriate in a steaming hot bath, my cares

drifting away with the steam. Am I pioneer material, I wonder?

Monday 15th
Market and then fencing once more – No peace for the wicked!

Tuesday 16th
I had just finished the fence and let the pigs out this morning, when the Attestation Officer came to test the calves. I had kept them in especially for this test. When he had finished injecting them, sticking his awful needle into their necks, he asked for the rest of the herd, Clarabella. Horror of horrors! I had let her out as usual, thinking she was already attested. 'Oh, I didn't know you would have to test her too,' I excused.

'Yes, it must be the whole herd,' he replied. The whole herd – three calves and a cow – I couldn't help chuckling inwardly.

'She is only up in the top field and she comes when I call.' I boasted. He followed me trustingly up the bank into the 'fog'. Not a sign of a cow, in spite of my anguished calls. 'Of course, she only mixes with attested cows,' I assured him.

'I'll test her on Friday when I come to see if the calves are all right,' he said, looking at me rather queerly, and, justifiably annoyed, he strode off down the bank to his car. I was wandering disconsolately homewards when I heard something behind me. Sure enough, there was the truant. 'Oh, Clarabella, how could you?' I asked, dissolving into laughter on her neck.

Wednesday 17th
A lovely day – funny we seemed to have most of the fog in October.

The pigs have started getting out of my new fence – I knew it – I patch up one place and they get out in another. Why will they never get back? But this was a small thing today compared to my worry over Clarabella. Milking time, no head peering over the top. A visit to Old Binks' revealed no Clarabella. Leaving word with Mrs Binks that she was missing, I hurried back to Granny. It was dark and I hate to leave her alone especially in the dark. Should I ring up the police? Was she wandering down Sutton Bank, in dire danger of being run over and causing an accident in the dark? I was very worried and waited impatiently for Old Binks to appear. I knew he would come. He works at the Forestry now and has to milk when he gets home. He arrived eventually as I was getting almost desperate.

'Deean't worry,' he said cheerfully, 'ah saw 'er this efterneean, up at t'top o' t'leeane; she can't 'ev getten far bi noo.' We left Granny with the two dogs for company and set off up the road. My nerves were already taut, and Torty, jumping on my shoulder in the darkness, just about finished me off. She is very affectionate but, after all, there is a time and place for everything. We chased her home. I didn't want to lose her up the road. It was a lovely frosty night and soon the stars appeared in the blackness of the sky, giving us enough light to see our way. In other circumstances I would have enjoyed the walk but I was anxious. Coming to the top of the lane we turned off into another lane on the right and a large dark shape loomed up at the sound of my voice. It was my darling Clarabella. She was almost as glad to see us, as we were to see her. We set off back, Old Binks at the rear and I in front, with a hop, skip and jump out of the way of her horns. What a party! I was so relieved I could have sung for joy. Was she blown? It hadn't occurred to me, but Old Binks examined her and assured me she was all right, so he wouldn't have to make a hole in her hide to let the wind out. He milked her too, for which I was very grateful, as she was almost bursting at the seams. He is so much better and quicker than I am. Soon she was comfortably bedded down for the night. We repaired to the house for hot cups of tea and post mortems, Torty purring snugly round the back of my neck. What should I do without Old Binks? I just couldn't. He is like a rock. I ask him to put the head on the fencing hammer. 'Why, it's ommost like a blacksmith's shop wi' all these 'ere nails and junk, whativer 'ev ya bin daeing at it?' It takes him only a few minutes to fix it. He really seems to enjoy all these adventures. Clarabella's days of wandering are over and done with. This settles it once and for all. A safe field for that lady from now on.

Thursday 18th

I seem to have fixed the bracken pigs for the time being. Now Jemima and Co have started again. I was very surprised to see them coming along the road in a row, looking very pleased with themselves. I put them back in and watched carefully. They must have got bored with jumping fences; now they are scaling the walls. The field is on a much lower level than the road, and I always thought the wall was a sufficient fence on that side. It isn't! They made straight for the lowest part of the wall, near a hawthorn tree and, one after another in a follow-my-leader line, they scrambled up the wall and back on to the road. Loose stone walls have always been my pride and joy. I have always admired the miles and miles of stone stretching over Yorkshire, and wondered how they had been built. Now was my chance to find out – the hard way as usual. The stones are very heavy and of different shapes. I find it difficult, and I know for certain that when I have built up one part of the wall the pigs will find their way up another. What have I done to deserve this?

Monday 22nd

Market Day once more. We are in a low cloud. The railway lorry came to deliver the pig meal, and he couldn't turn round. The stack yard is getting very sticky and it was quite impossible, the lorry wheels churned up huge ruts making matters worse. In the end he decided to reverse all the way up the road to the gate. Reversing any distance is a tricky business, at any time, but up our road it is doubly dangerous. One false turn on the corner and the lorry would tipple over into the field. It was a nightmare both for him and me, watching him out of sight, praying silently. He made it. I must get in plenty of food for the winter; soon they won't want to deliver it. I can see it coming. Old Binks has suggested the egg room as a storage place for the winter foodstocks. I think it is a jolly good idea. At least the rats won't get at it there, and he says he will carry it out for me, as I want it.

Tuesday 23rd

A lovely day – I was busy at my masonry, superintended only by Wodgie and Brutus, and watched in the distance by the unrepentant pigs, when the Hunt suddenly appeared over the White Horse hill. Hundreds of hounds, or so it seemed, streaming, baying down the slope. Horsemen in pink and a blowing of horns. I scrambled up the wall, dislodging one of my recently built stones in the effort, grabbed Wodgie and Brutus by their collars and, fairly dragging them along, rushed up and put them in the cowhouse, slamming the door and peering over it from the inside. I had visions of my pets being torn to pieces by the hounds. Breathless from my exertions, I must have looked a picture of guilt when a very elegant young lady in riding habit and bowler hat appeared with a huntsman. I am quite sure they suspected me of having the fox hidden away in the shed behind me. Another huntsman was galloping across the pig field. He jumped up my wall, but it was a 'four-faulter' as the horse's hooves caught my masonry and toppled it back into the field. I groaned aloud; to him it was just a dislodged stone or two – nothing at all – to me, it meant at least another hour's hard labour. The noise receded, the scent apparently going the other way. Peace reigned once more, or almost, Clarabella had become quite frantic and was tearing round and round in her field, almost hysterical. I calmed my pregnant darling down, put her in her familiar stall, gave her some dairy nuts as compensation, and went back to my wall.

How lovely the Hunt looks – on Christmas Cards!

Friday 26th
Today was fine, so we went off to Scarborough and boosted our morale, Granny buying a new hat, and I a tweedy Danimac with hat to match. We had lunch with Ida and exchanged gossip. Granny recounted all our adventures and the antics of all the animals. I must say Ida was glad to see us fit and well. She worries about us. I said we just daren't have a cold or anything, so take precautions. Granny looks marvellous. She has a new bloom about her. I'm sure it's because she is the boss once more and head of her own household, thinking now about making Christmas puddings and a cake. It does one good to get out; we return refreshed. What a storm is raging now. It whirls around the house, but we feel safe within our solid stone walls.

Saturday 27th

Today has been terribly wild.

I cleaned out the chickens, a very disagreeable job, but so necessary. To get the smell out of my system, I climbed the bank to the three Scots pines, followed by Wodgie and Brutus. The wind was terrific, it almost blew me in half, but I enjoyed it, and came back by the Valley of Lost Horizons. Clarabella caught sight of me and followed me home. What a pet she is!

Granny and I were sitting together this evening, one at each side of the fire, in our usual places, chatting sleepily, thinking it was almost time to go to bed, when, suddenly, there came a peremptory knocking. It was very loud; we were petrified, looking at each other with white faces. Who could it be? Who on earth could knock as hard as that, anyway? I tremble now when I think of that first shock. It is the unknown that frightens. Recovering slightly, I realised that if it had been someone at the back door, Wodgie and Brutus would have barked furiously. As it was, with the scullery door shut, they had merely growled. We waited with baited breath, picturing 'bodies of two lonely women' etc. There it was again 'ratata-tatatat' – it just couldn't be human, but it seemed very close. Screwing my courage to sticking point, I crept into the egg room and peeped nervously through the window. All was isolated as usual – not a sign of a soul, only the sighing of the wind as it came round the corner of the house. The noise seemed to come from near the chimney. By this time we had realised that it just couldn't be human, and the colour came back to our cheeks. We went off to bed, listening for the knocking. Granny heard it, at intervals, through the night, but I am afraid I was too tired and fell asleep almost as soon as my head touched the pillow, only pausing long enough to ask God to take care of us and all my babies.

Monday 29th

Market Day and a lovely day too. We went to see Mr Roberts, the Secretary of the NFU. I asked his advice about an electric fence. I wonder, will that keep my pigs in? Discussing the question of my heather, he arranged to come up and measure it for me.

I have ordered nine fruit trees; wonder when they will be here.

We are still being haunted by our 'ratatatatat' and it wasn't until we were coming back from market that I discovered what it was. I had removed all the sections of wood from the side of the house, but this had made no difference. Now I knew. The chimneys of Bracken Hill always come into view first, now one of them looked distinctly drunk. It was the cowl which had slipped, giving the chimney a definite 'hat-over-one-eye' look, very jaunty. Every time the cowl revolved, it thumped on the chimney pot. No wonder we had been scared. In the gale it had been swung round at such a pace as to give out a thunderous 'ratatatat'. The unknown was plumbed. Although we were no longer frightened, we had been puzzled.

Tuesday 30th
My old enemy the south-east wind came – the Aga went out!

December

Wednesday 1st
A notice came in the post; the fruit trees were at Coxwold station. What on earth were they doing there, as I put Thirsk as my nearest station, on the order form. We had to get ready and go down to Coxwold to collect them. It's time they were planted. Granny enjoyed the ride, the sun was shining and it was very pleasant. We returned with the sack-bound, straw-filled parcel balanced between us and sticking out at the back of the van. The trees were very carefully packed; I sorted them out for planting and put them away until the morrow. Cox's Orange Pippins, Laxton Superbs, Bramleys, Victoria Plum, Pear and Cherry. Glowing visions of a lovely orchard and me lying under the shady trees on a sunny day, dreaming!

Thursday 2nd
Planted three trees. What a hard job it is. The ground is so stony, it is almost like a quarry. Will the trees have sufficient soil to survive? Dalesfoot Prince is a friendly fellow, but I can

90

manage quite well without his help. He jumped over to see what I was doing and I had to pull up a stake and the wire to get him back in. Why can't he mind his own business? I have been most careful in planting the trees, two Cox's and a Bramley. After I had filled in the holes and stamped down the earth firmly, I wrapped sacks round the trunks up to the first branches and put chicken wire round the base. See what the rabbits will do to that?

Friday 3rd
Terrific gale blowing. The straw stack has blown over. I can't carry a bale, only trundle it, so that's another job for Old Binks. I joined the British Agricultural Traders' Association when we were down in Helmsley. I can collect the necessary foodstuffs when we go to market on Fridays, then as Old Binks has taken to coming over every Friday, he will carry it into the bins for me. I can do this, but have to half-empty every sack into buckets and then carry the rest. This is such a waste of time.

Old Binks was sitting having his cup of tea as usual, after doing his goodwill tasks, when the cowl on the chimney started up. Nearly jumping out of his chair he exclaimed, 'Whativer's that?'

'Oh, it's only our old friend,' we told him nonchalantly, quite hardened by now to the interruption.

The Aga is roaring red – it will go out.

'Think on,' Old Binks reminded me, with a fine disregard of the cost, as he left. 'We might 'ev a rum snawy winter, get yon stuff ordered and stored i' t'egg room.' I promised.

Saturday 4th
A showery day, but in between the showers I planted the rest of the trees. Thank goodness that job's done. They won't run away or cause me any worry. They'll stay put. Granny thinks they look fine.

I am fixing up the stable for Toby. He is coming to join us tomorrow.

Sunday 5th
A message for Old Binks came over the telephone, so I had to

91

go over and deliver it. In the afternoon, I was just putting the finishing touches to the stable, when Old Binks and the boyfriend appeared with Toby stepping daintily at the end of a halter. 'Ah've brokken 'im ti lead,' Old Binks explained. ''E'll be orl-reet noo, he's hobbut young yit, nut quite two.' Toby gazed at me with his soft brown eyes and I lost my heart once more. He is dark brown, shaggy and truly beautiful, taking after his pony mother rather than his donkey father. He pokes his head over the door and belongs already. Visions of Toby, drawing a little cart full of stones to build a wall round the garden and keep out the rabbits, flit through my mind.

The pigs got out again, but this is now routine, so it worries me less and less.

Monday 6th
We have had a reminder today that winter is approaching. It was very nippy this morning when we went to market. With all my precious plumbing, I decided I had better be on the safe side, so bought some solder and fluxite – just in case I have to 'wipe-a-joint'. Have ordered tons of food, sufficient I hope to last a couple of months, and I shall not use it until I am forced. Bought an electric fence. Surely this will put a stop to these pigs of mine. Funny, they might have known. When we got back there wasn't a pig out of place.

I have wrapped the outside tap with straw and sacking to try to prevent it freezing.

Vivienne is coming home early as there is flu at school. We shall have to collect her on Friday. Bit of luck really.

The wallflowers are still alive and thriving – Granny has green fingers.

Wednesday 8th
We had a very hard frost last night and the outside tap was slightly frozen this morning. What a good job I wrapped it.

All the winter food came. The lorries drove right up to the back door and the men carried the sacks through the kitchen into the egg room. It had started to snow, so Granny put papers down to try and save her floors. What a mess, but

92

what a relief. It is snowing hard now – everything is white over. Luckily I fixed up snow shelters for the outside hens. My efforts are very puny, but it will stop the snow driving in. Tomorrow I must do as much work as possible to make it easier on Friday.

Friday 10th
Got up at six this morning. It was quite dark and the Aga was out. Wouldn't it just? Granny made a fire in the kitchen and boiled the kettle, while I did the necessary chores. The hens were most surprised to be let out so early and in the dark too. They were reluctant to leave their perches, so I left them to it and just filled up their troughs with mash and scattered the corn. They would find it later. The pigs too, wondered what was the matter, but food is food after all. Clarabella was lying down. She, too, was rather sleepy, but dairy nuts in her trough, she stood up, and, patient as always, quietly chewed and watched me ruminatively, while the milk spurted rhythmically into the clean white pail.

Vivienne likes to be collected early, but most of the other girls had gone by the time we arrived. The porter put her trunk in the back of the van, and we were off. A whole month's holiday. Lunching at Ida's afterwards we dashed back to try and get the Aga going. Too much of a down draught, it just won't go. Old Binks came over, it being Friday night; he couldn't do it either. The dogs recognise his cheery whistle as he approaches the house. How thoughtful of him to whistle and let us know who it is.

Vivienne claims her own bed again, so I have to sleep in the big room. It seems strange, but it is lovely to have her home again. She is very thrilled with Toby and takes him for his customary walk.

Saturday 11th
What a help it is to have Vivienne at home once more; she has taken over the hens, and I have been trying to get the Aga going all day. Finally, after tea, I managed it, but I was thoroughly fed up of it by that time.

Two pigs got out too, but with Vivienne to turn them, it was an easy job to get them back in.

It is snowing.

Sunday 12th

White over with snow, the view has changed, but has an added beauty. I rushed downstairs this morning to the scullery. The Aga was warm. The water had been warm, but I couldn't be sure that the Aga had stayed in until I touched it. The kettle was on the simmering plate; it would soon boil. I went out into the white morning to feed my pets. Vivienne isn't very good at getting up in the morning; I find it easier to do the work, than wake her up.

We both took Toby for a walk. On the way back we took off his halter and let him go free. He shook himself and set off at a terrific gallop tossing his head from side to side and sniffing the breeze. I expected at any minute he would take to the air, like Pegasus. He is delightful and full of spirit, enchanting us all, except perhaps Wodgie, who has given him a very wide berth since he tried to stamp on her. She just couldn't understand why anyone should want to hurt her, and luckily she wasn't harmed.

Monday 13th

What a shock this morning when I opened the back door. There, in the yard, stood a large white boar pig, a monster. I shouted for Vivienne. She was down in a jiffy, no sluggard when I needed her, and we chased him down the road, away from the house and my precious 'Welsh' darlings. Visions of my pedigree floating away on the air and large white crossed Welsh, appearing. I left him to Vivienne and returned to the chores. She chased him all the way down the hill, slipping and skidding on the icy road. What a brave girl she is, she didn't hesitate! He was really huge, much bigger than Dalesfoot Prince or Simon; good thing he didn't see either of them, he could easily have killed them. I think he must have come from the piggery down the road. I am still quivering at the thought of what might have happened.

It was quite tricky driving to market, but we got home safely. The bracken pigs were out, and Simon. I jumped out of the van; 'Simon,' I said, in a very severe voice, 'what are you doing out, come along.' Looking very sheepish – if a pig can look sheepish – he hung his head and followed me like a lamb back into his pen. He looked so dejected, just like a naughty boy.

Wednesday 15th
All the snow has gone, thank goodness. We can do very well without it. Filled in licence application form for Dalesfoot Prince. It's a bit late, but I have only just found out about it. Forms – Forms – Forms!

Toby did his galloping act again. I love to see him, he looks the essence of freedom.

Friday 17th
When we came back from Helmsley, Jemima was with Dalesfoot Prince. Clearly, she doesn't know the rules, and, if she did, she wouldn't care. Nature is her guide.

Got the Highway Code and have sent off my form of application for a driving test, my visitor to Great Britain licence being out in February. When Old Binks came over I told him about Jemima and we decided to move Dalesfoot Prince out of temptation's way, until such time as he was licensed. Easier said than done. It was dark and, with the aid of a torch we got him out of his pen into the garden; but would he go through the garden gate? Not he! He ran round and round the apple trees, two of us trying to turn him. Then he was out of the beam of the torch, we could only trace him by his heavy breathing. 'Ger on wi' tha, thoo greeat daft gummuck,' Old Binks panted. That was the nearest he came to swearing; at least audibly. I have never heard him swear, what a gentleman! If ever he had an excuse, he had tonight. It was midnight before we got the boar safely in a sty, Old Binks half carrying him in the end. We were both exhausted and bathed in perspiration. Granny and Vivienne had gone to bed at their usual time, so I made a cup of tea and, refreshed once more, Old Binks went home, very late. What will his wife say, I wonder?

Saturday 18th
David rang up to say that he was on his way home. He had been sent down early because he had broken the rules and

stayed out late at a party. He was walking from Thirsk, when he got a lift from Sutton to the top of the lane. This is really no punishment, he is very pleased to be coming home early. I had to come the 'heavy Mother' stuff, and gave him a stern lecture on 'rules are made to be kept – not broken', but really I am very pleased to see him. Now we can get the electric fence up.

Sunday 19th
Got all the Christmas parcels ready. Hope Panchi will like her scarf. I have always felt a little guilty about the time she thought I had given her one of mine, and I had only asked her to press it. Still she won't mind it being late for Christmas, she is a Dyak and doesn't really observe Christmas, except for accepting presents. What a lot of cards Vivienne sends, they cost a fortune! David doesn't send very many, but our sum total is quite staggering.

I have daubed some brown paint on Jemima's forehead, to distinguish her from her sisters, although I'm sure she will soon look quite different. What hairy things pigs are! It was quite a business getting the paint on to the skin. It soon won't be visible through the mud, but still!

Monday 20th
The shops look quite Christmassy. David wanted me to buy an icing set so that he can make a really professional job of icing the cake. I will not buy an icing set. I am firm – he is furious. 'It's a luxury, and luxuries are out' I state firmly – 'But it won't cost 5/-', he points out reasonably. I am very unreasonable about this, and I don't really know why. It's just one of those silly little things. I am stubborn about it.

WINTER

If Winter comes, can Spring be far behind?
Shelley

December

Tuesday 21st
I wonder why Vivienne is such a dreamer. She took the dogs
for a walk today, remembered to bring back wood for the fire,
but lost her rain hat, which I had insisted on her wearing. She
hasn't even bothered to look for it, that's what makes me so
furious. It is the little things that seem to irritate me these days.
Am I getting to be a nagging old woman? I hope not! Am
determined not to buy another rain hat at this stage of VC's
school career. Don't suppose she ever wears the thing at school
anyway – wouldn't have worn it today if I hadn't made her.
Still it's on the inventory, so I'll have a look for it. She is trained
to bring back wood anyway, that's one step forward, or is it? In
her short life she has left a purse in Rangoon, a watch in
Singapore and her school hat on a BOAC plane. What can I
expect really?

Wednesday 22nd
The postman is getting later and later every day. I feel sorry for
him, having to trail all the way up here with parcels. He looks
very well on it, and seems very cheerful. I suppose it's his job,
and it is nicer to walk up grassy fields than on hard wet
pavements in a town.
　Went looking for Vivienne's rain hat and found it. Amazing really, she couldn't remember exactly where she had
been.
　We don't want the Aga to go out over Christmas and

97

it has been smelling sulphury lately, so David and I cleaned out the flues. What a mess, but it will go better for it.

Old Binks came over and culled out two hens for our Christmas dinner. He showed me how to tell if they were laying. There must be quite a few not laying at the moment.

Thursday 23rd
Taking the dogs with us, we set off, this morning, to look for some holly to decorate the house. I have had in my mind, for some time, a particular holly bush in the lane, as a handy source of supply. The bush has disappeared. How can a holly bush disappear? I am certain it was there about a month ago, or was it my imagination? I am beginning to think anything can happen here. We searched up and down the lane, and in the end had to get our holly from a tree in the bracken on Old Binks' farm. Vivienne and David are going to do the decorations.

David put the almond icing on the cake. Tomorrow morning early, I am taking Helen and the boyfriend to Ampleforth to catch the 7.30 a.m. bus.

David is quite sure the house is haunted. He doesn't say much about it, but I can tell. If he weren't so tired at night, he would have difficulty in getting to sleep. As it is, his head no sooner touches the pillow than he is off.

A gale sprang up just as we were going to bed – a real gale, like the one we had before, when the cowl was dislodged. I was slipping thankfully between the sheets when there was a terrific crash. I listened, no more crashes. I can't do anything now – see about it tomorrow.

Friday 24th
Up before the crack of dawn. What a morning! It was starting to snow. I went out into a dark yard and nearly fell over some broken tiles. Getting the van out, I turned on the headlights and behold, our friend the 'knocking cowl' had finally toppled over, taking half the chimney with him. I couldn't see the extent of the damage done. It would have to wait until I got back. Roy and Helen met me at the gate and we made good time to Ampleforth. The snow was driving across the moor,

clogging up the windscreen wipers. I had to be directed as I didn't really know the way, but made a mental note of it, for my return. When I got back, I found that some of the tiles had gone through the attic roof and the sky was plainly visible through a very large hole. What a good thing it wasn't a bedroom!

Vivienne's precious film books were in jeopardy. She has removed them to the farthest corner of the attic, where there are no floorboards. Why so far away? Nobody would want to interfere with them, I'm quite sure. As a temporary measure I put a sack over the hole in the roof, went straight down to the study and rang up the builders. 'Yes, we'll come, as soon as we can,' they promised. I shall have to be satisfied with that, I suppose.

David has iced the cake without an icing set, and it looks very nice too.

Saturday 25th
Christmas Day – we did only the essential – had a lovely Christmas dinner, listened to the Queen's Broadcast, ate far too much and took Toby Jinx for a walk. He is now Toby Jinx, it just came to me one day, when I was having a few words with him, and I think it suits him. I do so love to see him gallop.

The sitting room looks very festive. We had crackers and paper hats, and then sang Christmas Carols round the piano at the top of our voices. David plays quite nicely. He would play better, if he had attended all his lessons, but boys will be boys, I suppose!

Sunday 26th
Christmas over for another year.

Old Binks came across and he and David put up the electric fence in the big field. Poor Wodgie was too inquisitive and her sensitive nose touched the wire. She did howl. Well it works anyway. This'll fix 'em, I thought. Over cups of tea, we discussed my driving test at the end of January. I am studying the Highway Code in my spare time. Old Binks is very sceptical about it. 'If it's yon woman tester, you weeant pass, she fails iverybody t'fost tahme,' he comforted me. 'But I've just got to pass,' I wailed.

Daddy is being transferred home. 'Do try and get back home before the pigs start farrowing,' I plead.

Monday 27th
David is going to a party, we had to take him to Thirsk station to catch the train. When we got back the pigs had got through the electric fence. It was ticking away, but the wires were on the ground. My pigs just aren't like anybody else's pigs. How is it that when I travel the countryside I see a thin wire separating luxuriant growth from sparse grass, with the animals on the right side of the wire? I put Jemima and Co back inside the wire and fixed it, very gingerly, I must admit, and waited. I could see them plucking up their courage, then, nose down, squealing madly, they dashed under the wire. They won't come back through it though, even for food, and just stand crying plaintively at the other side of the wire, and the electricity pumps away into the earth. It's very strange but the only time I have seen my pigs subdued, is when there is a high wind. I can't believe that 'pigs can see wind', but it certainly affects them in some strange way.

Tuesday 28th
Lovely day, David rang up to say he was bringing Tony and Olly back with him. Tony was on his way home to Scarborough, but Olly is going to stay for a few days. What big fellows they are. A lovely sight to see them walk into the yard and a lucky thing we have plenty to eat. What appetites!

Wednesday 29th
My forty-second birthday.
The licensing officer arrived and approved Dalesfoot Prince, licensing him by stamping a crown on his ear, and giving me a certificate. The officer was enchanted with Bracken Hill and said that when he came to license Simon in February, he would bring his wife with him and show her the view. Another milestone passed – Dalesfoot Prince is now fully adult and capable. We let him out of his sty, intending to put him through the gate into the big field to his wives. He was so thrilled at being free again, he forestalled us by taking a flying leap over

the wall into the field, in full view of his astonished audience, Olly, Vivienne, Granny, David and me. I bet he had a shock when he landed, because the level of the field is much lower than that of the yard, but he didn't break any bones, and soon forgot about it in the fussiness of his wives. What a good thing he jumped into the right field. Something right for once!

I decided to 'insulate' the pigs while I had plenty of help. I have been reading all about keeping pigs warm in the winter and as the field shed is rather lofty, I think it is necessary to make it warmer. We put cross bars across, about three feet from the ground, covered them with old chicken wire, and piled on it all the old hay and straw I could spare. Six little piggies are now cosy for winter. We gave them a couple of bales of straw for bedding and they are quite happy. Funny to watch them. They root about amongst it and then collect a mouthful and take it into a corner and make a bed. Almost like a bird making a nest.

We had just finished tea when there was a great commotion in Simon's pen. Going out, we found the bracken gilts had broken into his run. Usually they were safe in bed at this time, so they must have been desperate. Olly thought chasing them out was great fun. I didn't mind either, with all these hefty people to do the rushing around. By the light of torches, we eventually got them safely back to bed and things returned to normal once more.

I am sleeping in David's bed now and he and Olly are sharing the big bed. I know that David feels Bracken Hill is haunted. I was fast asleep when I had a very strange sensation. Waking very suddenly, I heard a funny buzzing sort of sound. My heart stopped and then raced on, thudding twenty to the dozen. I crouched panic-stricken, under the bedclothes. Nothing happened, but the noise kept coming intermittently. Eventually I realised it was the wind in the telephone wires, which are fastened to that corner of the house, but I must say it is very scaring. I shall have to explain to David.

Thursday 30th
The deep litter again – what a headache this is. I wish they could go out 'free-range', but I just daren't; the old fox has his eye on us. While I had two strong boys to help, we decided to

go down to Robert Thompson's in the village for some sawdust. What a craftsman he is! Before we collected our sawdust, we watched the craftsmen at work and I inspected furniture, pulpits and pews, all beautifully made. On each of them is carved a small mouse; 'industry in quiet places' is the meaning of it, I believe. I must get something of his, sometime. I wonder if the hens will appreciate this craftsman's dust. We had quite a load and with our combined weight, I decided not to take our rum corner, but to go up the White House hill. This is steep too, but not quite as bad as ours. We stopped at the top of the hill and looked down at our domain. It looks quite a farm now, pigs, cow, calves, hens and a mule. We shouted at the dogs; they heard us but couldn't make out where the sound came from. How bewildered they looked!

Vivienne and Olly took Toby Jinx for a walk, while David and I cleaned out the trampled deep litter. Poor David, he is the 'man of the house', and has to do all the dirty jobs.

No sign of the builders yet.

Friday 31st
The hairdresser asked all about my family as Vivienne and I had our hair cut. We told her all the amusing incidents and finished off the weekend shopping. In the afternoon I superintended the enlarging of Simon's pen. What joy to watch someone else wield that heavy hammer and get somewhere with it.

New Year's Eve. A windy New Year's Eve. No cowl protection from the wind and only half a chimney; the smoke swirled down in the midst of our celebrations. Toasting 'Absent Friends' we saw 1955 in, with the window and back door wide open, smoke pouring out and David and Olly drinking cocktails of Raisin Wine and Cider. What a mixture! But they look no worse for it. My memory turns to the many fancy dress Balls I have attended in the romantic tropics, in the dim and distant past.

January 1955

Saturday 1st
Sent off tax form for the van.

102

Olly fell downstairs. What on earth was he doing jumping down backwards! Nobody told me about it. I discovered by accident, as so many mothers do, by listening to what was going on. What next? He seems all right, and he and David went off shooting grey squirrels; the NFU are paying 1s a tail. The only thing about a grey squirrel that is at all pretty, is its tail. The animal itself is just like a rat, but the tails are lovely. We have two in the sideboard drawer now.

David is changing girlfriends, I know the signs. He thinks he can hide it and this evening he was trying to write a letter. Chewing the end of his pen, he covered the front of the pad and the blotter with his signature 'David J Welburn'. 'Can I help you?' I inquired innocently.

'I am trying to write a letter of condolence, as some relation of Skoff's has passed away,' he answered. What a lame one! Did he expect me to swallow that? Chuckling inwardly, I suggested certain suitable sentences and went back to my knitting. After much pen chewing and more signatures, the letter was completed. Needless to say, he didn't let me read it, but I was not at all surprised when he decided to return to Richmond with Olly.

Monday 3rd
When we went to market, we took the boys to the station and I gave David strict instructions to hurry back, as we had a lot of work to do. Olly thanked me for his holiday, I said it was nice to have had him, and they were off. We returned to do our shopping and then went back home to the chores.

David is taking Biology at the Girls' High School, I think this has something to do with his visit to Richmond. Some time ago he put a crust of bread in the bottom cupboard, hoping to grow some mould. I looked at it today; it is as hard as a board, but not a whisker of mould is to be seen. Next to it is an old pair of shoes, green over. No accounting for it, is there?

Wednesday 5th
Toby Jinx enjoys his daily walk. He follows us sedately at the end of his halter and when we turn for home just loves his gallop. David is staying away too long. I am beginning to feel

annoyed about it. He rang up and I told him to come home, so he is coming tomorrow. Am I spoiling his holiday? Sometimes I think I have too much work to do and can't enjoy the children as I should. Oh, well!

Vivienne helped me to 'insulate' Simon. He was very fussy welcoming us into his house, and kept getting in the way. It will keep him warm, if we have a hard winter.

Thursday 6th
David returned. His new girlfriend's name is Sheila. As I guessed, she is a pupil at the high school and takes Biology.

My mushroom project is no further advanced. I read the instructions and it needs small straw. David, Vivienne and I set to work on a bale of straw, in one of the disused pig sties, using a pair of scissors and a pair of clippers. I held the straw while David used the clippers, and Vivienne cut hers with the scissors. What a task! However, with determination and perseverance, we eventually surveyed a whole bale of straw cut up into small pieces. By this time, we were thoroughly fed up and tired. What industry! But how much easier to get some 'chop' on a threshing day.

Have ordered some turnips and potatoes. David and I are collecting the potatoes and the turnips will be delivered soon. I must have something to fill up the gaps, meal is so dear. Old Binks is going halves with the turnips, as he wants some too.

Friday 7th
Leaving Vivienne in charge of Granny, or the other way round, David and I set off for the potatoes, taking our own sacks. We felt we could manage 10 cwt as it is a 10-cwt van. Returning we were faced with Sutton Bank. Looking at David I said, 'Shall I take a run at it.' 'No, just take it at a steady pace,' he advised. I wish I had taken a run at it; just as we were getting near the top of the one-in-four, nearly to the flat bit, the accelerator didn't respond. All our straining forward couldn't help the gallant little van. She coughed, then konked out, starting to roll backwards down the steep hill. I put the brakes on, got out and said to David, 'Back it slowly down and have another go without my weight.' I really hadn't the nerve to back it downwards but David had. Luckily there was

no other traffic about at the time. He slowly and skilfully backed it down, until he could get another start. Being a very good driver he soon had the van on the level stretch, I returned to the driving seat and we crawled safely to the top, and then down to our homestead. What a comfort David is! He hasn't a nerve in his body. I was really scared. 'You're a marvellous driver, Mummy,' he said. What a morale-raiser! Now we have ten sacks of potatoes stored in the barn. Contrary to all the best advice in all the best books, I am afraid the pigs will have to eat them raw. I have no time to boil them.

David's cases are almost packed, just a few last minute things. I shall certainly miss him; Granny too, she enjoys the company of these young things.

Monday 10th
Leaving the crate of eggs at market on the way, we took David to school, early, much to his disgust, but Granny doesn't care for driving in the dark, so we just have to go early. Vivienne's turn next.

The calves only go out on fine days now that it is getting colder. I thought Toby Jinx might be company for them and Clarabella, but they don't appreciate his playfulness at all, at least I hope it is playfulness. He chases them madly round the field, so, different fields it has to be, and he can gallop to his heart's content without upsetting anybody. I must say I couldn't help laughing, as he chased the bovines; cows are such ungainly runners and he is so very graceful, but, after all Clarabella is pregnant, so now he reigns in solitary glory, and sleeps, snug and warm, in his own little stable, waking at daylight to poke his beautiful head over the door and watch me do the rounds. Will he ever earn his keep? As a very special treat, I occasionally give him some of Clarabella's dairy nuts and a carrot or two. He responds by giving me lots of love; money can't buy that. He is a darling and I love him. His nose is so soft, black and velvety.

Thursday 13th
Vivienne's turn to go back to school. It was terribly frosty; I dashed round all the taps; they weren't frozen which is a great relief. The breath steamed out of every animal in a white

filmy cloud. Vivienne went round to say goodbye to everything. All dressed up in school uniform, ready for departure, she had to give Toby Jinx a last petting and a carrot. She slipped on one of the frosty cobblestones and nearly went for six into the muck-heap. Just saved! Phew!

The breath almost freezing on our lips, we got the trunk into the back of the van, tucked VC under a rug on the back seat with her tuck etc, got Granny safely in, and, with a rug stretched across our knees and tucked in, we set off. I had cleaned the windscreen, but our warm breath froze as it hit the glass. No defroster on this van. What a nightmare journey it was! I just couldn't keep the glass clear and only managed to just see where I was going. There is very little traffic at this time of the year, thank goodness, but it is nerve-wracking just the same. I called at Ida's first and dropped Granny to thaw out. Ida had a bright idea to rub salt on the windscreen and I deposited Vivienne at school safely, and returned. Granny was recounting our adventures with great gusto, her cheeks pink, her eyes glowing. She looked marvellous, the picture of health. Looking at her, I was touched. How grateful I am to her for her companionship. She is a tower of strength and, although the responsibility of all my undertakings is now weighing heavily upon my shoulders, I have only to go indoors and see her and realise that she is behind me in everything, with a word of encouragement when I feel tired and depressed, and the house is spotless. She forgets nothing, our shopping lists are compiled by her and it is really amazing how she thrives on all this work; even the isolation doesn't seem to trouble her. She loves the radio and all the personalities and she can recognise any voice. Occasionally she is a little disappointed when she finds a photograph of one of her favourites does not quite come up to her expected standard. 'Oh, I didn't think he would look like that,' she says disconsolately, but recovers and goes on admiring and recognising voices. We rely on the BBC for our only means of entertainment these days, and follow 'The Archers' very closely. They seem like real people to us by now. Granny is a very wonderful person, and I owe her a great deal. I know that Ida worries about us, but we just daren't have a cold or be ill, so I think we don't, but we certainly take every precaution.

Friday 14th
The turnips came. They were dumped in the field near the gate, as the driver was afraid to come all the way down. The frost hasn't given. I went round all the taps this morning and they were all right, thank goodness. Old Binks is coming over tomorrow to help me get the turnips in and take his half back home.

Brutus is a naughty boy. He has discovered that if he puts his paws on the Aga, he can reach the things on the clothes line. This morning, we discovered one of Granny's best pinnies on the floor all chewed up. Now he is to be banished to the cowhouse. I have made him a nice straw bed, and he can have his Bonio at bedtime as an added incentive. I can't really be cross with him, he just smiles at me. His lips part and a smile appears from long silky ear to long silky ear, all his lovely teeth showing. Enchanting! I can't resist it, and he knows it.

Saturday 15th
What a day this has been!

Old Binks came over with his tractor and trailer to load the turnips. I have never felt so cold in all my life; it was perishing, the drizzle froze almost before it touched the ground or whatever it touched. It touched me and Old Binks and the tractor and the turnips. I held the sacks open whilst he filled them and I gradually froze, layer by layer. My coat, scarf and gloves, with a coating of ice, were like frosted glass which scrunched when I moved, and looked very pretty, but ooh! it was cold. We managed to get one load down before lunch and decided to leave the other until afternoon. I was so thankful to get inside and thaw out. Washing my hands, I groaned aloud as the life came tingling back into my fingers. Then I listened to hear if the water was running into the tank. Not a sound; I ran as much hot water as I dared, and rushed upstairs into the cylinder cupboard to listen again – not a drip. It was up to me! What did plumbers do? (forget their tools – no time for jokes). I got a chair, clambered on to the cylinder cupboard shelves and, using them as a ladder climbed up into the loft. Granny handed me up a lighted candle and some old newspapers and sacks and I went to it, in the dim cold enormous loft. What a huge tank it is! I have never seen such a big one. With some difficulty, I lifted the cover. It was only about half full of water, and the ball tap was solid. I put the candle flame under the pipe I guessed to be frozen, and waited with fast-beating heart. First one drip, then another, then a cracking of ice in the pipe and a gushing of water from the ball tap. I had caught it in time. *I had won!* The sense of victory went to my head. I forgot the cold and only felt a warm glow of triumph.

'I've done it,' I shouted down to an anxious Granny. 'Well done,' she replied. Wrapping the offending pipe thoroughly with old papers, I tied sacks round it, dragged the lid back on to the tank, and gratefully descended. We almost danced a jig. This time we were saved, surely we can never have such another frost. Bubbling over with my success, I had to tell Old Binks as soon as I saw him.

'Noo then, ya needn't 'ev dun it, Ah'd 've fixed it for ya,' he said, 'I know you would, but I thought it might freeze harder, before you had the chance.' Somehow, sacking the turnips didn't seem quite so hard, and we finished in good time for milking.

For some time now I have been pulling hay out of the stack, and consequently it has assumed the shape of a mushroom. I couldn't climb on top of it, as it is rickety and anyway all the top hay is sopping wet. Pulling hay out this way is no easy task; why do I always have to do things the hard way, I wonder? How a 'time and motion study' expert would shudder at this waste of time! He wouldn't tackle such a stack, he'd write it off, but I can't afford to do this. Clarabella has the tastiest bits, not very tasty at that, but she doesn't grumble, then the calves the next best, and poor old Toby Jinx has the leavings. Now they can have a bit of variety in their diet with the turnips.

Sunday 16th
The chickens are growing up and will soon be coming on to lay. This afternoon I saw Brutus and Wodgie playing with something up in the field. They were tossing it up in the air. It looked strangely like a chicken. I raced up, but was too late; it was dead. This will never do. I have seen Brutus chasing the

chickens before, but I can't risk losses like this. It's a bad habit. I wrote to David and told him that if I couldn't cure Brutus, he would have to be given away or destroyed. As if I really could! But something must be done. My heart is very heavy.

Monday 17th
Decided that I ought to have an extra calor gas cylinder on hand, just in case we have a bad winter. So far it isn't too bad, but you never know, so we brought one back with us from market.

I was feeding the hens tonight, when Brutus started chasing round the wire again. Granny came out and shouted at him, then she had a very bright idea. 'Throw the tin at him,' she advised; I acted promptly and threw the old Minto tin; it didn't hit him, but rattled its way towards him across the yard. Terrified he cowered on the back door step, trembling in every limb. Now I know what to do. I only have to rattle a bucket or brandish a tin and he sits on the back door step as good as gold. I hurried off to write to David and tell him that his Bruty was saved. What a relief! It would have broken my heart too.

Wednesday 19th
A heart-broken letter from David, saying, 'I know you've never loved Brutus as much as Wodgie etc.' I wish I had waited and he wouldn't have been worried, but now he knows his pet is saved.

Am feeling very nervous about my driving test tomorrow. Shall have to be up early to get everything done before we go. What shall I do with Granny?

Thursday 20th
A bright clear day. I hurried through the chores, settled Granny in the van, we tucked the rug round our knees, and we were off. Butterflies in my stomach, I decided to leave Granny at Woolworths, where she could walk round in a warm atmosphere, and reported for the test. This didn't seem much out of the ordinary, but I *failed* – I just couldn't believe it. 'What have I done wrong?' I agonised.

'We are not allowed to discuss it,' she replied primly, and

handed me a form with crosses on it. 'Cutting my corners,' 'Inconsideration to other road users.' I just couldn't believe it, after all my driving experiences. My heart was in my boots. What shall I do now? I picked Granny up, broke the sad news, and bemoaned my fate all the way home. I had a sympathetic ear. 'I think you are a very good driver and I always feel safe with you,' comforted Granny. Praise indeed, and balm to my wounded spirit. My current licence expires in February, what shall I do then? I have applied for another test as soon as possible, and have also written a pathetic letter to the authorities explaining my position. Could they possibly extend my current licence for three months, or waive the L plates, as I have 12 pigs, 1 cow, 3 calves, about 250 hens, a mule, 2 dogs, 2 cats, and last, but by no means least, my elderly Mother, reliant upon me, etc?

Friday 21st
Old Binks came over as usual. We went out to fix the electric fence.

There was not a sound of life save that acme and sublimation of all dismal sounds, the bark of a fox, its three hollow notes being rendered at intervals of a minute with the precision of a funeral bell.

Thomas Hardy

That describes it exactly. We wandered slowly down the field in the darkness inspecting the fence at intervals with the aid of a torch. The night fitted in with my gloomy mood as I recounted the details of my driving test. All he said was 'Noo then, what did Ah tell ya, she nivver passes onybody t'fost tahme, but nivver mahnd, ye'll dae it next tahme.' Somehow, it seemed quite a joke to him, but I am still seething with disappointment and frustration. What's the good of this electric fence anyway? The pigs just ignore it.

All the gilts have been served. I have marked them with various distinguishing marks, X, Y, T, etc, but now they all look alike. Jemima is getting rounder; I expect that Buttercup, Daisy and Topsy will have their babies about three weeks

110

after her. I'm not so sure about Susannah. Thank goodness Daddy will be home before April. I can't face the thought of all that farrowing. I never have any difficulty in examining any of the pigs. They are very friendly, in fact much too friendly at times. They mill around me and take a gentle nibble at my coat or wellingtons. I don't really care for these love pecks, their teeth are very sharp.

Monday 24th
We got back from market to find that Dalesfoot Prince had decided to take unto himself another wife, in fact two, Hyacinth and Twinkle. Now I just don't know where I am. I had intended them for Simon. Nature! Simon will be licensed early in February, but he is growing up rapidly.

Tuesday 25th
Another complication; Simon is very much in love with Miss Otis. He must be, he stayed out all night and when I went to the barn this morning, I found he had made himself a nest at the foot of the haystack, and was snuggled down, grunting comfortably. I rooted him out of it, cruelly, and took him back to his pen. What's the use? Nature is much stronger than I! I have marked Miss Otis with a different coloured paint. She doesn't seem to mind.

Wednesday 26th
Simon out with Miss Otis again. I give up, but I speak to him sharply and his feelings are hurt.

Friday 28th
Old Binks' cheery whistle heralds his approach once more. I make a full report on all the doings of my animals and receive his advice, which is to let Nature take its course. I don't appear to have much option. He also empties the van of its load. Now that I have been calling at BATA for some time, I have got to know the man who loads the meal for me and we talk pigs. He has some too, so we compare notes. I feel very knowledgeable, almost a farmer! Old Binks entertains us with his stories of the days when he was walking an 'entire' horse. I remember seeing these stallions walking from village to

village when I was a child. 'An' then there was t'tahme when Ah was at t'Co-op,' he goes on. We hear some of the stories time and time again, but they are amusing.

'And if thoo ivver daes owt for nowt allus dae it fer thisen'' what a gross misconception of a Yorkshireman!

My letter about my driving licence has done me no good. The first authorities passed the buck to another authority, and now I am quoted 'Section x, subsection y' etc, and given no help at all. I can see the red tape, like bindweed, twining round their umbrellas and bowler hats, choking all reason. I am going to break the law, quite deliberately, without a qualm. I have done my best! This is against all my upbringing, but I can see no alternative. When my licence is out, I shall get a Provisional and drive as before. What would the policeman in Thirsk think, if I suddenly sprouted L plates, anyway? He'd have a fit, and would certainly start asking questions. As it is, he is used to seeing us every Monday. We are part of market day.

Saturday 29th
It must have been a false alarm with Susannah. She is in season again. I don't have to worry, Dalesfoot Prince will see to that. Jemima is now showing her pregnancy.

February

Tuesday 1st
Must remember to send off David's birthday present tomorrow. He will be seventeen years old on Thursday. I know what he will get, first of all, his driving licence. He can hardly wait.

The turnips have made a welcome change in diet for all. They have also made more work for me. I can give Clarabella, Toby Jinx and the pigs, whole ones, but not the calves. Oh no, my Jonathan, Percival and Ferdy, have to have theirs chopped up, or they might choke. No turnip cutter with its luscious cubes pouring out. No! the hard way, as usual. Spreading a sack on the ground, I choose the nicest turnips and cut them up into small pieces with the spade. This is quite a hard, messy job, but the result is worth the trouble and the calves

112

really enjoy the juicy morsels. I am right-handed and my 'fencer's elbow' has returned.

I have no trouble getting the hens in now. They don't like the cold nights and go to bed about 4.30. I leave the Tilley in the deep-litter shed until six as an encouragement.

Tuesday 8th

A lovely day.

The licensing officer came to see us again, bringing his wife, as promised, to see the view. I am glad it was sunny. Although wintry, the view is still very lovely. It was duly admired, Simon licensed and I proceeded to show them round. In their car, they had a dog, which barked continuously at Wodgie and Brutus, who were rather bewildered by this, never having seen another dog since their puppy days. Toby Jinx was in the field, but came galloping down at the sound of my call, and, catching sight of Clarabella, jumped over or tried to jump over my fence. He is no point-to-point jumper, and down came the fence. My poor fences! I thought I had fixed that one at last, but Toby Jinx was so pleased to see me, I had to forgive him. He nuzzled me and I was lost. Giving him a carrot, I put him back in the field and got out the heavy hammer. Fencing my bête noire!

Simon, duly licensed, sporting his crown, joined his wives. It was easy. I just said, 'Come along, Simon,' and he followed me. What is that I read about vicious boar pigs! Feeding is simplified now, only two lots of pigs.

Wednesday 9th

The snow came. It drifted down gently and clothed the trees in fairy garments, muffling the hills in a great white silence, which could be felt. Somebody was certainly plucking a goose, up there. It just goes on and on. I hope it clears before market day. I don't like driving in snow.

I have sent off for my Provisional licence.

Friday 11th

The snow is still coming down. It is getting deeper and deeper. I think we must reconcile ourselves to the fact that we are snowed in. I cannot get the van out of the garage and the road is blocked anyway. My days are ruled by the snow; clearing paths to the cowhouse, barn, deep-litter shed, coalhouse and hen yards. Every morning the same routine and the paths are getting slippery. I daren't let Granny out, as we can't risk a broken leg. What a beautiful world it is! The pigs don't seem to want to get out in the snow, that is one good thing. It is watering that is the problem. I thaw the outside tap and carry water to all my pets. We have a hosepipe but it doesn't fix to the tap properly and, anyone coming out of the back door is treated to a shower, so as all the surplus water freezes and makes things dangerous, I have to carry buckets. All the animals are inside now – snowbound. Clarabella drinks twelve whole bucketsful – I just couldn't believe it at first – six slippery trips from tap to stall twice a day. She dips her great head to the bucket, 'slrrpp', all gone in one gulp. The calves drink less, but there are three of them, and Toby Jinx I take to the water as I always take him out for exercise. He sniffs the clear air and gallops around to keep warm. I fill up the pig troughs after first breaking the ice. The hen fountains are now taken in at night-time. Hens must have lots of water, and I can't afford to have their fountains freezing up.

All my inside plumbing is working, as yet. I go the rounds every morning when I get up. What a lovely house to keep out all that frost. The snow piles up on my sack over the hole in the attic roof. The builder now has a legitimate excuse not to come up. He just can't get up. All sorts of receptacles catch the drips as we can't allow water to soak through the kitchen roof. It all adds to the variety of life.

Sunday 13th
Have made a note that Genevieve and Bluebell were served by Simon today. The snow covers everything and there isn't a thing we can do about it. No market tomorrow, without a doubt. From this height, the village looks like something out of a picture book. I can see traffic moving along those roads, but then the snow plough patrols down there. Have written to the children saying they had better stay at school for half-term. I can't possibly collect them, unless there is a decided change in the weather, and it doesn't look like it. The

wallflowers have disappeared; the rabbits have eaten every one, but the fruit trees are saved by their sacking and wire. I feel rather sorry for the rabbits as there isn't a blade of grass or anything to eat anywhere, and the old hungry fox lies in wait.

Monday 14th
No market. A good thing I got in a few extra crates for the eggs. They'll have to wait until next week.

I fixed some more snow shields on the hen houses to stop the driving snow. The hens are getting very bored. I put straw in the yard for them to scratch in and hang turnips on the wire for them to peck but they just huddle and look miserable and have started feather pecking. In the morning, after a fresh fall of snow, they flutter about trying to lift their legs high enough to walk in the deep snow. It is very comical, but I am not amused when I see the silly things pecking the feathers off each other's backs and actually eating them. They are no longer my black beauties, but now have horribly patchy pink backs and starkly naked parson's noses. 'Try daubin' 'em wi' Stockholm Tar,' Old Binks advises. We try. I catch them, one by one, and Granny does the daubing. Hope it works.

The postman brings us yeast and Granny makes bread. I make butter, we have eggs and chickens, and we live like lords in our splendid isolation. The rabbits are getting weak from lack of food and the dogs, seeing them outlined against the snow, catch them quite easily. Granny paunches them, as I can never bring myself to do that, I skin them and the dogs are fed. At least we shall not starve. I shall soon have to start on my winter stock in the egg room. How relieved I am that it is there.

Tuesday 15th
Having some important letters to post and the postman missing us for one day, I decided to walk down to the village. Granny was very sweet about it, but I could see she was nervous at being left alone. She had the dogs and I promised not to be any longer than necessary, and set off, following in the postman's footsteps. In the deep drifts I couldn't stride as far as he, so had to put both feet into one hole. The snow is

115

very deep in places. It was a struggle and when I was through the drifts I had to brush the snow out of my wellingtons; nothing quite so uncomfortable as wet legs and feet. It was a lovely day, the sun shone, turning the fields and woods into fairyland and I really enjoyed my walk. I posted the letters, called at the village shop for necessary groceries, and then went to see the butcher. We have a very strange connection with the butcher. I have never seen him before today, but apparently he was a great friend of the previous owners of Bracken Hill and he is the other party on our telephone party line. Some arrangement had been made that all local calls are put on my bill, I can never understand this, and shall have to get it altered. After all, I very rarely make local calls, as I know no one in the district, and we have only rung up the vet about three times, and I have a bill of 15s odd. Finding no one in the butcher's shop, I had to go to the house. The butcher didn't know me, either, but when I explained my errand, he very kindly took me to the shop and cut off a piece of meat, my share of the bill! Trudging back home, up the woods and fields, with my load, I worked out a good letter to send to the post office Telephones. I'm glad I have told the postman never to bother coming up with just circulars. It is very tiring, but Granny was so pleased to see me back, and the dogs so excited, I soon forgot my weariness.

Please God, don't let anything happen to either of us.

Friday 18th
David rang up, very worried about us. The snow isn't so bad in Richmond. He wants to come home for half-term, even if he has to walk from Thirsk. I just can't risk it; he may not be able to get back and he is safer at school. Very reluctantly he agrees.

Old Binks came over, as usual, to see if we were all right, and what a night! He was like a snowman, but doesn't seem to mind at all. 'Ah'll bring t'auld mare ower timorrow wi' t'snaw-ploo, an' clear a bit o' that stuff for ya,' he tells me. We are very grateful.

Saturday 19th
It has been snowing all night. Old Binks came over with his

116

snow plough and 't'bairns'. They enjoy this weather, their faces rosy with the cold air. It has made a bit of difference, but we are definitely snowed in. He took away one crate of eggs to go on the bus to market on Monday.

There is nothing like a blazing log fire for cheer, on days like this, and we appreciate all those logs I sawed up, now.

Sunday 20th

A blizzard. I have never really been in a blizzard before, but I just had to go out and feed up and get the coal and coke in. It blew from the north-west, cutting me through like a knife, obliterating everything in its passage, filling nostrils and eyes and getting in all the cracks. Muffled up to the ears, I struggled round. Now I have at least some vague ideas of how Scott must have felt in the Antarctic. Not an animal or bird put out its nose or beak. They knew better. Milking had to be done and I groped my way to and from the cowhouse, this time without my Torty. Even she has enough sense to stay in near the Aga in this weather. What a wonderful sight from the comfort of the kitchen; the ploughshare drifts form and actually overhang the top of the bank. There isn't a sound.

Vivienne's headmistress rang up about lunch time to say that Vivienne is always in tears; will not eat or sleep, and would I talk to her, if she rang up in the evening. I agreed readily, and assured the headmistress that we were all right, even though we were snowed in. I waited impatiently for evening, suffering with VC. Poor darling, she is so worried about us, being snowed up and having all the work to do. I had to point out to her that if she worried about me, I was going to have an added worry, worrying about her and it would just be a vicious circle. I assured her we were fine and all the pets were fine, told her one or two of the funny incidents and she laughed, albeit rather shakily, and promised not to worry. I said that when I knew she was being cared for at school, I was not worried about her. She promised to be a good girl and not to distress anybody. I am very touched by my children's devotion. Have I, I wonder, made my letters too dramatic? I must lighten them in future.

Monday 21st
Got up very early this morning, got everything done, then started off across to Binks'. Calling for Mrs Binks, we set off together down the fields to catch the market bus. The crate of eggs was in the bottom shed. She gave me a hand with it and we waited by the side of the road in the still cold morning. The roads were icy but the snow was pressed down hard and the traffic could run. The market bus came, the driver loaded the crate of eggs into the back and we set off for market, picking up people and goods on the way. How helpful these country bus drivers are, nothing is too much trouble. Our driver delivered the crate at its destination and put in two more empty crates, for return. I rushed around doing the necessary shopping, bearing in mind that I should have to carry it up home. Returning, I left the bus at the point where the postman comes up the fields and literally followed in his footsteps, my shopping bag getting heavier and heavier at every step. I do love these hills, but!

Granny was so relieved to see me, it was quite pathetic, and the dogs were ecstatic. I was glad to be back too, the thought of my dear mother up in that lonely house cut off from everything is very disturbing. Cups of tea and an account of how things looked at the market, and life went on much as usual. 'They are snowed up in Scotland,' Granny remarks, 'and helicopters have to drop supplies.'

Tuesday 22nd
Shrove Tuesday and Granny made pancakes. No one can make pancakes quite like hers.

There was a letter from Boon Kong written for Panchi. Poor old Panchi can't read or write, but she could certainly deal with her money. Letters in polite stilted broken English are fascinating. She is thrilled with her present, and hopes I will return to Sarawak. I can't imagine what it feels like to be hot.

As I was out feeding up the animals, a helicopter came over, hovering above us for some time. I was very tempted to put out a large C but decided that my supplies will probably last out. Surely this snow can't last for ever. There is nothing but snow, snow and more snow. The pigs' troughs are all frozen solid now, I just can't thaw them out any more. The pigs will just have to eat snow if they are thirsty; there is plenty of it. They seem fit enough and have no desire to roam. At least that's something to be thankful for. Toby Jinx is the only one allowed any liberty apart from the dogs, who love the snow. He wanders around when I let him out and has a gallop but, even he doesn't roam far away, but follows me around as I go about my work.

The house is still hugging to itself all its lovely plumbing and keeping at bay the icy fingers of Jack Frost. Another thing to be thankful for. 'Count your blessings,' my father always used to say. I am trying!

Wednesday 23rd
Nothing happened.

Friday 25th
It hasn't snowed today, and the sun has been shining. As I had some letters to post, I thought I would try to get up to the pillar box at Hambleton. I set off up the field by the short cut; the snow is quite thin here; it has drifted into the road lower down. Arriving at the lane, I found that the snow was level with the stone walls. I walked along the top of the wall to the top of the bank and then saw a sight which I shall never forget. Wave upon wave of driven snow, like silver plough-shares glimmering brightly in the sun. I was lost in admiration; how beautiful it all was and how silent! It must have been about six foot deep so, deciding that discretion was the better part of valour, I retraced my steps, returned to tell Granny all about it, and set off down to the village leaving Wodgie as company for Granny, but taking Brutus with me. He was delighted.

Sunday 27th
The world is still a world of snow, snow, snow. Today I took Granny for a little walk as far as the cowhouse, holding tightly to her arm, so that she would not fall. She used her walking stick and we managed fine. The paths are very slippery now, I just daren't let her walk out by herself.

The poor rabbits are nibbling all the bark off the trees. How

119

glad I am my fruit trees are protected as the snow is very deep in the orchard.

Old Binks came over with his sledge and the mare and took two crates of eggs. The eggs are really mounting up. What price fresh eggs now! I shall have to go to market again tomorrow. I wonder when we shall be able to get out the van.

Monday 28th
I made another long and weary trip to market. The roads are almost clear in Thirsk as it has been thawing slightly, but there is very little change in our situation. It will have to be a big thaw to make any difference to us. I notice the water has been running off the roof, the snow has melted there.

March

Tuesday 1st
March and we are in the grip of a mighty frost. The water, dripping from the tiles, has frozen into beautiful icicles, iridescent in the gleaming sunshine. What a picture! I just had to take a snap of it, and am only sorry I haven't a colour film. At the back of the house I broke off an icicle but just like a sword, about three feet long. What a frost! The water is still running through the veins of my lovely house and only the outside tap has to be thawed out; this is comparatively easy and routine now.

Thursday 3rd
I am getting a bit restive in this solitude. I just had to find out what it is like in the outside world. Is there an outside world, or is it just snow, snow, snow? I decided to ring up my friend in Surrey. Olive is such a comfort; we have been friends since our schooldays. No matter how long we are apart, whenever we meet, we start again where we left off. She was horrified to think that we had been snowed in for so long and duly sympathised. After exchanging all our family news, I went to bed cheered up considerably. There is an outside world after all.

Saturday 5th

I think it thaws a little bit every day and then freezes again at night. The roads look almost clear in the village. How frustrating! The days are so sunny that I have decided to start digging out the road. What a task, but something must be done. Granny has only had two short walks and it seems weeks since we had a real market day. Soon I was cutting into the frozen snow, throwing it to the side of the road in large chunks, like outsize ice-cream blocks. The sun shone down warmly, and I discarded my coat. There I was, a glamorous female in blue slacks and yellow sweater, and not a soul to see! I love to make river courses with the water draining away, remnants of my childhood, I suppose, but I can't leave it in pools to freeze. I have dug out most of the drifts, so do hope it continues thawing. There is still snow on the hill up to the gate, but it is not too deep, and I just can't do everything.

The haystack is finished – Old Binks had to push it over for me, he was scared it would fall on me, and now it has all gone. He is going to let me have some of his good hay.

Sunday 6th

The weather is so lovely and the sun has melted the snow in the field. I decide to let Clarabella out for a short while; she has been in so long. Old Binks warned me that she would be frisky, but I didn't realise she would be quite so giddy. She frolicked, kicking her heels in the air, almost like the cow that jumped over the moon! 'Clarabella dear, do please be careful,' I cautioned, visions of a very pregnant cow measuring her length on the cobblestones of the yard, passing through my mind. She ignored me completely, keeping up her jigging until she was safely in the field. Then she settled down to chewing and munching the flattened unappetising grass.

The Stockholm Tar hasn't done any good for the black beauties, so Granny suggested mustard. We painstakingly plastered each of the culprits with the yellow mess. I hope it smarts! I think it has only added spice. Probably they enjoy feathers with mustard. I come as near hating these hens, as I can come to hating anything that breathes.

Monday 7th
A fine but cold morning, a slight frost but no more snow; we decided to have a shot at getting to market in the van. Feeling rather scared, it must be admitted, we set off, negotiating the first part which I had dug out, quite safely, and were rounding the corner on the last little rise when the back wheels began to spin and we skidded to one side. Granny was frightened and I was too. I stopped, she got out and decided to walk to the gate and wait for me and I had to let her go, bravely walking off in the snow. Praying that she would not fall, I turned my attention to the van once more. It was worse than ever and suddenly the rear offside wheel slipped off the edge of the road. This was too much. I put the brakes on, stopped the engine and got out. Finding a big stone I propped this under the offending wheel and set off for the gate. Granny and I walked slowly and carefully back home and the eggs stayed in the van. She resumed her household tasks and I returned to the scene of disaster with sacks and a spade. Maybe I could dig it out and get a grip with the sacks. I have never, never felt so helpless! All I needed was just one little push from behind and there was no one there to give it to me. Never have I felt so alone! I spent all morning trying and then decided to wait until I could get Old Binks to help. Couldn't afford to run the battery down. He called on his way home from work; he had seen us from his vantage point on Hood Bank. 'Ah saw t'van set off and then get stuck, then yah figure set off for t'gate and then another yan foller up, and then Ah saw two foaks cum on bac,' he explained. 'Ah guessed what 'ad 'appened, so 'ere I am.' I have never been so pleased to see anyone in my whole life. We went up to the van, I got in, started her up, he gave me just one little push and off I went to the gate, turned round and restored her once more to her place in the garage, as easy as that! Never shall I forget that feeling of futility and aloneness. We don't mind Old Binks keeping tabs on us. We welcome it and his cheery way of tackling every problem.

Wednesday 9th
Really I think this has been the most miserable day I have ever spent. It is certainly the most miserable day we have spent at

Bracken Hill. A cold thaw came creeping over everything, chilling us to the bone and the Aga went out. A damp down-draught caused the kitchen fire to belch out clouds of horrible sulphury smoke from the coke we were striving to redden. We had to light the sitting-room fire and let the kitchen fire out. In the midst of all this Mr S from the Gliding Club came down, with a friend of his, to see if we had survived the horrors of the snow. They had been snowed up at the top for as long as we had, so we had something in common, but they hadn't a solid stone house to protect them from the cold. They couldn't help with the Aga; it was just a matter of time. I was very concerned about Granny; she wouldn't sit in front of the fire, but insisted on doing the work as usual and we were both blue and pinched with cold. Eventually, with red hot coke slowing turning duller and duller as I rushed, with sulphur fumes choking me, through the hall and kitchen to the reluctant Aga, we managed to get it going, and soon we were warm again, and I had a luxurious hot bath, just to show! I think the thaw has come to stay and the snow is leaving us; reluctantly the last vestiges hide in the crevices of the rocks and sheltered spots. We are released at last!

Friday 11th
It is still cold but we ventured to Helmsley. I found no difficulty in getting out this time, the road is quite clear. Across the moor, the drifts are still piled high at the side of the road, witness to the dreadful winter we have had. Granny was so glad to be able to walk around again, she was in great spirits. It was nice too, to be able to do lots of shopping without having to worry about carrying parcels. We called for more pig food at BATA told the tale of our experiences, were duly sympathised with, and returned to our fortress once more, refreshed in body and spirit, by communicating once more with the outside world.

God has certainly taken care of us through these fearful weeks.

We searched the garden for a trace of the wallflowers; not a leaf or a stalk, but the fruit trees are there standing up strongly, full of life. We can see by the rabbits' teeth marks on the other trees how deep the snow has been and we can hardly believe it has gone. The wretched black hens look even worse than before, so we try the Stockholm Tar treatment again; at least it is black and covers up their naked redness. I am ashamed of them, thoroughly ashamed!

I have had a letter from Nancy. She would like to come and see me for a flying visit. I haven't seen her since I was her assistant, teaching at the school in Sarawak. It will be nice to talk over old times. I arrange to collect her from Thirsk station on Monday, when we go to market.

Monday 14th
We got safely down to market, when it began to snow, large soft fluffy flakes, muffling all sound. Calling at the station, we collected Nancy and set off for home. The trees were beautiful; snow, inches thick, resting precariously on their stark branches. It was also getting thicker on the road. Sutton Bank loomed up in front of me and I was thoroughly frightened; I could feel the wheels skidding on the snowy road, could feel it through the accelerator, but dared not give a sign to Granny sitting there imperturbably by my side. We were up on the level stretch, then the nasty corner, then creeping inch by inch in time to my jagged nerves, up the last slope, my foot on the floor. The relief was immense, we were at the top! My heart came back out of my mouth, and I began to tell Nancy all about the lovely view, then chattered on, with relief, about nothing at all. We were home, the sun came out and the snow melted. We could hardly believe we had had any. Nancy has to go back tomorrow, but she is enchanted by the view and we have a good chat over old times. She is as pretty as ever.

Tuesday 15th
Took Nancy down to catch her train, then came back and moved the calves into the barn. Old Binks has made me a nice pen in there for them, so I know it won't break down. They seem a little bewildered but will settle down. The other day Old Binks said, 'You owt ti get t'farrowing pen riddy aboot a couple o' weeks or so afore she's due.' Jemima is due sometime early in April, and we decided her farrowing pen should be the loose box in the cowhouse. The calves have been in all winter making manure in there and it all has to be

cleaned out ready for Jemima. 'It's nae good, cleaning oot t'caulves ivvery day,' Old Binks had said, 'leeave' t'muck in and just add a bit o' straw, noo and then, they'll keep warmer that way.' Now I am faced with manure about two-feet deep, pressed down and running over! I have decided to ration myself to two barrowloads a day.

Thursday 17th
The weather is bright and sunny, and Toby Jinx is out in his field all day long, although sometimes he waits at the fence looking pathetic, hoping to have the run of the farm as in the snowy days. We always save him the apple peel and all cores. Wodgie gives him a wide berth but Brutus is braver; he hasn't been trampled on. Today, he sought out Toby Jinx in the field, and started to bark at him, egging him on. He needed little encouragement and set off after Brutus at his fastest gallop, the dog only just escaping those flailing hooves, by getting through the fence. I was completely helpless, the expression of surprise on Bruty's face had to be seen to be believed!

Spring is almost upon us and everything is beginning to raise its head, as the sap begins to rise. The daffodils are in bud in the field. How I love the spring flowers, they are so gay! I was looking round the garden, hoping the rabbits had left something, when I noticed the drains were blocked up. Getting out a long piece of wire I spent quite a time pushing it up and down the drainpipe. It is much better now, but I think there must be a blockage I just can't reach.

Saturday 19th
Vivienne's going-out weekend. We have to make a special effort, as she couldn't get home at half-term. 'And please bring Wodgie with you, I want Ange to see her,' she begs. I replied that Wodgie was growing and at the leggy stage, not half as pretty as she had been, in fact not pretty at all, but we would take her if that would make her happy etc. We couldn't take Brutus, he is such a bad traveller, but Wodgie loves sitting up in the van. Poor dear, she has big ears and spindly legs and huge paws. I suppose she will soon grow a shaggy coat, but at the moment, neither her coat, nor her tail is shaggy. Her pretty dumpling stage has gone, never to return,

and that is how VC remembers her; I know she'll be disappointed. Wodgie is, so truly, an 'in-between'. I suppose Vivienne has been swanking about her puppy. She was really disappointed and rather disgusted with Wodgie, as I had known she would be. Was this awkward gangling dog, her lovely cuddly puppy? I was immediately on the defensive. Poor Wodgie can't help it, she will probably soon be very lovely, just like her Old-English sheepdog mother. Vivienne soon forgot her disappointment, in her joy at seeing us safe and sound, after our imprisonment. We went back to Ida's, had a nice family afternoon and returned Vivienne to school once again. Her slight chilliness does not seem to have affected Wodgie, who is as affectionate as ever. After all beauty is only skin deep.

Sunday 20th
Toby Jinx has been very naughty today; I think, and hope, it is only high spirits. I was feeding the hens, followed by my faithful Torty, who is such an affectionate little cat, and, as she was walking along the hen run wire, Toby Jinx, who had been attracted by the sound of my voice, appeared to see what was going on, and, seeing Torty's tail waving about, he decided to investigate and have a bite. In a trice, Torty was hanging from his mouth by her tail, swinging from side to side squealing and spitting, claws extended to the full. I let out such a yell that Toby Jinx dropped her in surprise at my tone. She dashed away to safety and wasn't seen again until milking time when, there she was, waiting for me as usual in the cowhouse. I examined her thoroughly; she was no worse for her terrifying experience. I have had to speak severely to Toby Jinx, but he still has a mischievous look in his eye. He is so rough with everything except me, but he nuzzles me so gently, his velvety nose incredibly soft. He certainly knows on which side his bread is buttered.

SPRING AGAIN

March

Monday 21st

Market day once more. I am breaking the law, have been ever since I took the van out after the snow, as I am now on a Provisional licence, but who is to know? and I just can't help it. Or is it a crime just to be found out? We wave cheerily to the policeman on point duty, as we sail past with our eggs. He smiles and waves back as the sun which shines on the righteous and unrighteous alike.

We had only been back from market a short while, when I heard a rumbling and then a crash. Rushing out, I was just in time to see the wall at the corner of the pig field collapsing. The heavy stones fell into the field, missing all the occupants, luckily. Combination of frost and pigs rooting under it, I suppose. That will have to wait until Daddy comes home. I have put up a piece of wire to stop the pigs getting out, although it would be difficult to climb over that mound of stones. Knowing my pigs, I take no risk.

Tuesday 22nd

I decided that Jemima should come inside. I can't risk her in her present condition. The wall might have fallen on her. Her farrowing pen is not quite ready, but I don't suppose she will mind a bit of manure. I'll finish it off with her in it. Now she will have to be fed mash, sloppy, to help her milk. That's an extra. I think Daddy will be home before she farrows, as he is coming on 31st. My next driving test is April 1st, so I shall be able to put up my L plates when I go for it. How nice not to have to break the law.

I have reminded the builders about the chimney and they have promised to come quite soon.

Thursday 24th
The boys from Ampleforth College came over today for their ramble. Old Binks had warned me about this. 'Rum lads, they are an,' all he said, 'they leeave all t'gates oppen and climm ower t'fences.'

'I hope they don't knock down my poor fences,' I said, but was pleasantly surprised. They behaved very well. Swarming along at the top of the bank past the three Scots pines, they disappeared into the Valley of Lost Horizons and reappeared up the White Horse hill. Two small boys came down later with a viper they had killed in my field. They were thrilled with it.

I find it rather complicated cleaning out the farrowing pen with Jemima in it. She is so inquisitive and wants to investigate everything; she chews the barrow handles and the fork, and I have to devise means to keep her occupied. A turnip hidden in the far corner keeps her amused for a time, until she has demolished it, and I have to hurry while she is busy. Feeding time is also awkward, she is so eager for her sloppy mash; such a luxury after the dry stuff she has had and the pig nuts. It is hilarious. She hears me coming with the bucket and rushes at me. I open the gate, hide behind it as she dashes out into the cow stall, and, nipping smartly in I tip the luscious mess into her trough which is on top of the manure. I have only cleared it to ground level near the gate, so it is quite a step up. Jemima realises she has missed out somehow and comes snorting back. It is all right by then, the mash is safely in the trough and she can't knock it out of my hands, or spill the precious liquid in the muck. Today was funnier than ever; I wasn't quite smart enough and she came charging up just as I was emptying the bucket into the trough. Right between my legs, and there I was, sitting on her broad hairy back, laughing helplessly whilst she guzzled greedily. This expectant mother is very happy. She wouldn't swop her home for any of the latest farrowing pens.

Wednesday 30th
The builders have come at last, and now we have a whole chimney, and no hole in the attic roof. Just the day before Daddy comes back; it's ironic really. Vivienne breaks up

tomorrow for Easter. I am glad, as then Granny won't be alone when I go to York to collect Daddy. He arrives about two o'clock in the morning, an unearthly hour. Still there won't be any traffic on the roads at that time.

I look around, rather complacently, it must be admitted. I have brought all my family safely through a hard winter, no casualties, except a few sickly hens. I thrust the thought of my black beauties out of my mind. It doesn't seem to be affecting their laying anyway.

Thursday 31st
Anticipating no trouble or traffic, I set off about midnight, driving easily. On the quiet road coming into Easingwold, I spotted a light which seemed to be in the middle of the road. Slowing down I discovered it was; I was being flagged down. Oh no! it was a policeman, a young nice-looking village policeman. 'Oh please,' I prayed, 'don't let him ask for my licence.'

He seemed very surprised to see me, 'Where are you going?' he asked.

'Oh, I am meeting my husband at York station, he has just come home from abroad,' I replied, with my most charming smile, my heart beating sixty to the dozen (is that how criminals feel, at the sight of the law?). He shone his torch into the dark recesses of the van. There was nothing there.

'Have you seen any lorries or vans parked hereabouts?' he asked.

'No, only a few private cars by the council houses in Husthwaite.'

'Well, somebody has been stealing corn, and all lorries and vans are being searched,' he explained.

'Well, I couldn't lift a sack of corn anyway,' I sympathised, my conscience being quite clear on that score. 'I wish I could help you.' With parting smiles on both sides, I set off, with trembling limbs and a fast-beating heart to York. What an escape! I was overwhelmed at seeing my husband. 'You can drive,' I told him, 'I'm tired of breaking the law.' We didn't meet a soul on the way back. Bed, then my driving test.

129

April

Friday 1st

How I hate driving tests! My L plates glared belittlingly on the van as we set off for Northallerton, leaving Granny and Vivienne at home. It was the same tester. She failed me again, or did I fail? I don't know. I just feel that I never want to drive again. We had to collect David and Daddy made me drive to Richmond. I didn't want to, and felt miserable all the way there. I was cheered up by seeing David, and he drove all the way back. He handles the van confidently, but now I just don't know where I am. It must be nerves. I never seem to have trouble driving normally. Why can't I pass my test?

Sunday 3rd

Life now assumes a different tenor. Lots of people around to share the tasks, but it is different. Daddy will have to go to London for interviews and we have had long discussions. We have also tried to go through the accounts. He points out that Toby Jinx and the dogs are 'passengers'. But what 'passengers'! What on earth would I have done without them? I just can't think. Toby Jinx doesn't like Daddy, and avoids him whenever possible. Maybe he senses that he is a 'passenger'. I have relinquished the reins at Bracken Hill, but feel that I know best. A rather uncomfortable feeling.

The pigs got out today, just to show Daddy that I hadn't just been making it all up. He was livid, I am afraid he is rougher with them than ever I have been. I try to remonstrate but it is no use. He has decided to put Simon in a sty by himself. 'He won't stay in,' we tell him.

Monday 4th

After market, Daddy decided to put his plan, for Simon, into operation, and he imprisoned him in one of the empty pig sties. Simon stayed in, only a minute. He jumped up on to the door, teetered on the edge, then plunged out, looking very pleased with himself. 'I'll fix him,' said Daddy, and brought a plank of wood and nailed it firmly across the top. This took Simon rather longer to dislodge, but bump, thud, splinter,

130

and he was out again, his nose battered and a bleeding cut on his cheek. The children and I looked at each other with a 'told-you-so' look in our eye, but not a word was spoken. Simon retains his freedom.

Tuesday 5th
Daddy and David have cleaned out the cesspool, the drains had become clogged, and it was a job needing attention. It is nice to have men around to do these jobs.

Jemima is getting bigger every day. I think it will only be about a week now and the pigs keep getting out. Daddy and David fix the electric fence regularly, but it ticks away merrily pouring the current from its battery into the receptive earth.

The Tithe redemption is due again.

Daddy's leave will soon be over and we shall have to decide what to do.

Monday 11th
Jemima is due to have her babies. 'When t'milk shows an' she's uneasy and maks 'ersen a bed, ya can be shure it weeant be lang afore she farrows,' Old Binks has told me many times. Her milk showed today, and she began making a nest in the corner. I relinquished all my hopes of ever having any mushrooms, and gave Jemima some of the carefully cut-up straw, so that her babies would be com-fortable. At midnight she chose to start her operations. The Tilley hissing quietly in a distant corner, casting a faint glow on the proceedings, Daddy and I kept our vigil, whispering quietly together. This is the first time I have been present at any sort of birth, except my babies of course, and it is an experience I wouldn't have missed, although I don't particularly want to attend again. She seemed to have little trouble, just grunting quietly as at intervals, one-two-three-four-five-six-seven-eight-nine-ten-eleven pink silky piglets came into the world, sneezing their way to life, and staggering round to feed at Jemima's bulging teats almost immediately. One poor little soul was so weak and small, Daddy decided to put him out of his misery and then there were ten. What a lovely sight, Jemima lying on her

131

side with ten little pink silky piglets feeding hungrily! Our first babies. Vivienne will be thrilled.

I enter in the Pedigree Book: No. 77 – Jemima – piglets.

Tuesday 12th
The weather is really glorious. Vivienne is very thrilled with the babies and keeps going to see how they are getting on. They seem so tiny, but are quite strong on their legs now. Jemima is inclined to show them off. I agreed to let Vivienne feed her all by herself. It was Vivienne's big moment. Granny and I waited in the cowhouse admiring the silky babies, while Vivienne mixed the sloppy mash. She was rushing across from the barn to Jemima's pen, when she caught her toe in the stack net and measured her length on the ground, the mash spilling out around her, soaking slowly into the ground. The greedy hens, who were out at the time, made short work of salvage, and Vivienne picked herself up, her face streaming with tears. How often our big moments are spoiled! I soothed her down and said she could make some more. Drying her eyes, she mixed another bucketful, I gathered up the stack net and put it away behind the shed, and Jemima was safely fed and everybody was happy once more. I was very amused inside, but did not dare to show a sign of it. It was so Vivienne!

Friday 15th
Daddy and David have been 'plugging-muck'. They have borrowed Old Binks' tractor and trailer, and today, the tractor broke down, so now there will be repair job to do.

The weather is really glorious. An English spring – the hills are green with fresh bracken and the trees are once more dressed in their spring foliage. My fruit trees have survived that awful winter; it is a mere memory now, and there are signs of sparse blossom on one or two of them. What a triumph! I must have green fingers too, like Granny.

Rabbits are few and far between now, and the ones we do see have Myxamatosis. It is a dreadful sight, and we kill and bury them, when we find them in such a condition. The grass is growing strongly in the top field.

It is a year today, since we first saw Bracken Hill.

Saturday 16th

I missed Wodgie this morning and searched high and low for her. She never runs away normally. We found her at last; she was on her way down the lane to look for a husband, never considering Brutus in that light. She is on heat. Another of my problems has caught up with me. We shut her in one of the spare pig sties, tying Brutus up when we exercised her. She is very miserable and just can't understand it, and Brutus sits outside her door, trying to comfort her.

David goes back to school on Monday.

Monday 18th

Vivienne is 14 today. Daddy took David back to school, and we stayed at home.

Toby Jinx ran away. We searched and called – no frisky little mule to be seen. My heart sank. Vivienne and I went over to Old Binks' about teatime. 'T'bairns is shure they saw 'im ower at High Kilburn, as they cam heeam frae skeeal,' he comforted me, 'mebbe 'e's gone back ti 'is fost heeam.' I cheered up and when Daddy returned with the van, we set off for High Kilburn, Toby's birthplace. There he was grazing quietly in a little paddock. I was all for leading him gently home, I didn't care how far it was, and I was so relieved to have him back, but no! Daddy was not pandering to any mule. If I drove the van very slowly, he would sit in the back and lead Toby Jinx; it would be much quicker. I hated this. I couldn't get the right speed, it was either too fast or too slow, and Toby was not very good with Daddy anyway, and became a little stubborn, having to be dragged. I was quite sure I could have managed him much better. In the end I got my own way and Daddy drove off, muttering about mules and women. Toby Jinx, happy once more, sauntered slowly up the lane at the end of his halter, soothed, not frightened any more. Why had he run away? He had never attempted it before, was he unhappy at home? I just can't bear the thought of that gay little animal being unhappy.

Tuesday 19th

Today Vivienne decided to move her precious possessions out of the corner of the attic, as there was no longer a hole in

133

the roof. I was busy in the scullery, when there was a rain of plaster and, there, sticking through the roof, was a very long shapely feminine leg. Vivienne had out her foot in it again! I dashed upstairs and into the attic, but she had retrieved her leg by that time and was back on dry land. 'Have you hurt yourself,' I asked in great concern. 'Only a bruise and a scraped knee, Mummy.' I thought of what it might have been and tempered my scolding with mercy. One more job for the plasterers? I cleaned up the mess, rang up for the workmen, and waited for Daddy's reactions, Granny soothing her dear little VC.

Saturday 23rd
Topsy, Buttercup and Daisy are almost ready for farrowing. We made a pen for Toby Jinx next door to the calves in the barn and I helped Daddy make the stable into two pens, by putting up a gate halfway across. It's easy when someone else does the hammering, and I only have to hold. Toby Jinx is out all day, so he only has to sleep in the barn. The calves are out all day too, now that it is fine and they are growing up into strong young animals.

Vivienne goes back to school next Thursday. Shall have to get her things together.

Sunday 24th
I opened the back door to a lovely morning and a hideous noise. It was Toby Jinx saying 'good morning' – He couldn't see me from the barn as he had been able to do from the stable, and the noise, a cross between a neigh and a bray continued until I went to let him out. I'm sure he must have startled the calves with his greeting. I do so love this little mule, and I'm the only one who can do anything with him. I can catch him any time in the field or anywhere at all, but no one else can get near him. Strange, he is so gentle with me! He seems to have settled down again, although for a time we put him on a long rope and he didn't like that at all, so now he is in his old field once more.

Daddy has to go to London tomorrow, so I shall have to drive the van and break the law again. Oh dear! why can't I pass my test?

We put Jemima and her babies into Simon's old pen, moved Topsy into Jemima's sty, and Buttercup and Daisy now share the stable. More piglets next week! This time I think they can do it alone. It doesn't seem such a trouble. Dalesfoot Prince is much easier to deal with than Simon, so we put him in a sty and put Simon in the field with his wives. Susannah was left in the field, and I didn't care for the mixing of the two herds. There is sure to be some fighting.

Thursday 28th
Vivienne went back to school.

The writing is on the wall, we shall have to sell Bracken Hill. Daddy has been offered a job in England, and it is too good an opportunity to miss. I must face it. Bracken Hill can never support us in the manner to which we are accustomed. I think I have known it for a long time, and hidden it on that little shelf in my mind. Now we must face it, so we have decided to advertise in several papers.

The Min. of Ag and Fish Official came up to see if the calves qualify for subsidy. I think it was so far for him to walk, he qualified them so that he wouldn't have to come again, because I don't think Jonathan was quite broad enough. Still a cheque will be arriving in due course.

May

Monday 2nd
Buttercup and Daisy had their babies during the night without any trouble. Buttercup only has seven, but Daisy had ten and nine are living. She must have lain on one. Our family is increasing rapidly. Thank goodness I have a bit of help. Mash to mix, is much more trouble than feeding pignuts.

It isn't quite the same; Daddy has different methods from mine.

Tuesday 3rd
Mr T rang up from Leeds. During a very long conversation it appears that he has always wanted to live here and he is being retired early because of illness. We decide to think about it, and he will come up and see us.

Thursday 5th
Topsy has twelve babies, the most up to now. Jemima's family are well established and it is a lovely sight to see them on the bank in the sunshine. Big clumsy Jemima with her lively piglets. The little ones get through the fence and I am constantly on the alert in case Toby Jinx decides to stamp on them.

Friday 6th
Daddy's birthday. We decided to build up the stone wall which had fallen down. Even with a man to do the heavy work, this was no easy task. Simon was very nosy about the whole proceeding and soon became a nuisance. 'Go away, Simon,' I said in very sharp tones. He was cut to the quick; after all he was only trying to be friendly; his feelings were very hurt and he went off whimpering and wouldn't speak to me again that day. What a picture – a large boar pig whining at a word from a weak human female! One thing is certain, Simon must never go to market, nor Jemima, nor Clarabella, and definitely not my Toby Jinx. I hate the thought of any of them going to those cold unfriendly markets. I suppose I am not cut out to be a farmer. Animals matter too much to me.

Hyacinth doesn't look too good. She was fighting with Susannah; the other pigs seem to have accepted the fact that she is with them and that's that, but Hyacinth didn't like Susannah. She seems to be sulking and stays away from the other pigs; what worries us more is that she doesn't seem to be eating. I think we shall have to isolate her.

Granny has decided to go and stay with Ida for a while as I am not alone, but she will come back if I need her. She hates the thought of all the stock going. Things aren't the same at all.

Wednesday 11th
Winnie is coming over for a day or two bringing little Christine. We shall have to meet her tomorrow at the station.

Hyacinth is very sick, and I'm afraid we shall have to call in the vet as she won't eat anything at all. We have made her a pen where Toby Jinx was, and have fastened him in the cow stall next to Clarabella. We are very worried about it all;

Hyacinth isn't insured. That's one thing I never got round to.

As we shall soon be disposing of the stock I feel completely lost. All I have built up is now being dismantled and it is an unfamiliar feeling. There is a sadness about Bracken Hill and the weather is mocking me. It is marvellous.

Saturday 14th
Hyacinth died; our first and only big loss, and what a loss! The vet had a post-mortem to prove it was nothing infectious. It must have been the fight as she had twisted herself internally. Now eight little piglets will never know what it is to frolic in the bright sunshine. Hitching her carcase on to the van we dragged it up the field and buried her in a pit, building a cairn over her to stop the foxes digging her up. Poor Hyacinth! I feel very sad over her loss.

I think Mr T is going to buy Bracken Hill. Daddy has to start work soon, so we shall have to be selling off our stock, only keeping the babies until they are old enough to go as weaners. The rot has set in; I find I can't take much interest in the selling of the stock. Shan't mind about the hens at all, I know that quite well as I have never really got attached to them except of course, our Henrietta. Now Daddy has to find us a house near to his new job and everything must fit in.

We have had a visit from a very nice representative of the Forestry Commission. The matter will soon be cleared up now that we are selling the property, and will get the deeds.

Friday 20th
We have decided to let Mr T buy Bracken Hill and he will take over a few of the Rhode Island Reds just for his own use, including Henrietta. The postman is having some of the best pullets, and the rest went this morning. The poultry dealer who bought them said it didn't matter about the black beauties being no beauties, as they were only going for boilers. I hurriedly picked out Henrietta before she found herself in a crate on the way to becoming a boiler, and the rest were quickly counted and put into the van. 'How much do

you want for that little mule I saw in the field?' the dealer asked. My heart sank – it had come – the moment I had been dreading. Seeing my hesitation, he said, 'I'll give you £5 for him.' Would you believe it, £5, more than twice the amount I had paid for him – but it broke my heart.

'Are you quite sure he'll have a good home?' I asked in a trembling voice.

'Oh yes, he'll be a little boy's pet, when he has been broken in.' Visions of my Toby Jinx running round and round at the end of a rope flashed through my mind. What could I do? He would have to go eventually – I couldn't keep him.

'All right, if you can assure me he is going to someone who will love him,' I agreed, my heart aching. 'I'm sorry, Toby Jinx my pet, I had to do it,' I whispered as I brought him in that evening. He nuzzled me trustingly, wondering what it was all about. I gave him a large helping of dairy nuts as a balm to my injured heart, and went heavily indoors. How I shall miss that welcoming call every morning, hideous as it was! He is so singularly mine.

Saturday 21st
Old Binks came over and together we scrubbed Dalesfoot Prince, making him ready for market. He enjoyed this process and looked quite beautiful when he was finished. I hated the thought of market for him, but it can't be helped. Some of the in-pig gilts are going too and I have an awful sinking feeling in my tummy. I hate all this!

Monday 23rd
The cattle wagon came and took away five in-pig gilts, Susannah, late because of her false alarm, Miss Otis, Simon's first love, Bluebell, Twinkle and Genevieve. Dalesfoot Prince was also carefully loaded in, gleaming white and unfamiliar, and they were gone. The old order had certainly changed, yielding place to new. Less and less feeding now. We are weaning Jemima's babies and Jemima is now recovering her figure and spirits in the field with Simon. Thirty-eight little pigs now, and twenty-eight of them running around in the field with their mothers too.

Wednesday 25th
A day I shall never forget – the day I had been dreading! A very large cattle wagon arrived for a very small Toby Jinx. I had to catch him as nobody else could get near him. Putting on his halter, seeing him through a mist, I reluctantly led him into that horrible van. He didn't want to go in, even for me, and I had to coax him in with carrots, as I wouldn't allow him to be beaten. They penned him safely across the front with a gate. Such a very small mule in such a very large wagon! I kissed him for the last time on his soft velvety nose, and hurried stumblingly up the Valley of Lost Horizons. I had to be alone.

Friday 27th
We collected David for his half-term holiday. It was so nice to have him home again, his last holiday at Bracken Hill. The dealer from the top came down and we sold him the calves. Now Jonathan, Percival and our dear little Ferdy have gone off to be fattened for beef. What a depressing thought! I mustn't dwell on it or it upsets me.

Now that I have much more time to think, it seems worse and all my enthusiasm has waned; I just feel tired out.

We have sold Jemima's babies and are taking eight of them to a farm near Thirsk tomorrow. Old Binks is having the other two. Why did I agree to deliver them? I am no dealer, I am hopeless.

Roll and Molly are coming over to see us for Whitsuntide. I know that Molly will appreciate Bracken Hill and love our view. It looks as though we may have a railway strike.

Mr T is coming on Sunday to see Daddy about the details of buying the house.

Saturday 28th
Roll and Molly came. They are enchanted by Bracken Hill; the weather is marvellous, the air like wine. I can now enjoy the beauties of the place as I have lots of spare time but it is a bitter-sweet pleasure. We walked up to the Valley of Lost Horizons, as I wanted to show it off to Molly. It was beautiful, a mist blue of forget-me-nots, interspersed with the gold of

primroses. We hardly dared to walk for fear of treading such beauty underfoot, but the dogs had no such scruples; they chased each other madly in an excess of high spirits. The atmosphere of disintegration isn't affecting them at all. They are secure in the knowledge that they will be going with us.

David and I delivered the weaners to their new home. First of all he took the best two across to Old Binks as we are giving him one, and he is buying the other and then we went off with the other eight. Old Binks is also having Clarabella, when I can bear to part with her, and Jemima.

Sunday 29th
Roll drove the van and with Molly and I as passengers, set off to see Granny and Ida. It was a lovely day and a lovely drive. While we were away Mr T came to see Daddy and he is definitely buying Bracken Hill, although we are keeping the land at the top and the Valley of Lost Horizons, about fourteen acres. We shall also have a right to use the water from the spring. Granny feels very sad at the thought of the animals being sold, but we both knew it had to come. We had felt it for some time and I am relieved in a way, as I am quite tired out, having lost half a stone in weight. Neither Granny nor I would have missed the experience for anything. She was very pleased to see Roll, he is her seventh son.

Tuesday 31st
The railway strike is on and Daddy and Roll have to go to work. We took them to Thirsk in the van and then just hoped they would catch a bus or something. It is very worrying. We don't realise how important the railways are until we haven't got them. Now Molly has decided to stay a week and hope the strike will be over by then and she will be company for me anyway.

I am drying Clarabella off, gradually milking her less and less, as she will soon be having her calf, but not for me. She'll have to go before she calves.

When we delivered the pullets at the postman's house in Coxwold, we had a look round the village, and Molly was entranced. It is a very picturesque place, when one has time to study it.

June

Friday 3rd
Vivienne's half-term. As I was going to collect her, Molly decided to go with me and stay with her cousin in Scarborough for a while until she can get back home by rail.

Now there is only me and the two children at Bracken Hill – back almost where we started but not quite.

Saturday 4th
Vivienne has taken down all her film star pictures and the bedroom looks very bare without those smiling faces. We miss them.

Sunday 5th
Before we took David back to school, he said all his farewells to Bracken Hill, making a special journey up to the three Scots pines. Although they will still be ours, the house will be his home no longer. His next holidays will be spent elsewhere. He is very quiet.

Monday 6th
Took Vivienne back to school. Before leaving, she said her own private goodbyes to all that had meant anything to her, and we were off. Granny insisted on coming back with me, saying I must not be alone. I don't think I could face being alone – even though there is very little work to be done compared with what there was. It is not like old times. No Toby Jinx, very few hens, only Clarabella, Jemima, Simon, Topsy, Buttercup and Daisy and the youngest piglets.

I now start clearing up, taking down the fences I had such trouble in putting up. Daddy will be coming home most weekends, but I have a very unsettled feeling. I have felt like this before, when I have returned from abroad. I don't seem to belong anywhere! I don't like it!

Friday 17th
Mr T has brought some of his cherished possessions and is storing them in the study, as he doesn't want to trust them to the removers. He is thrilled at the thought of having Bracken

Hill, and is taking over the cats. This is a relief as I don't want to take them with me. There are all sorts of details to be sorted out and I try to remember everything, but feel dull and stupid, in spite of the marvellous weather. Is it reaction, I wonder?

Saturday 18th
Daddy came home for the weekend. Last weekend, he took the van with him, and he has now found a cottage, so we can agree on a completion date as we have somewhere to go. I have no feeling of excitement; I am just tired, so tired!

Monday 27th
Today Mr Banks collected Buttercup, Daisy and Simon, and the weaners and Topsy went to the dealer. Now the place is really beginning to look quite deserted and my heart is sad as I look around. I cut the lawns regularly as I have managed to keep them safe from the rooting of the pigs and they and the fruit trees are the only things worthwhile in the garden wilderness, so it is not complete desolation.

Old Binks came over after tea and took Jemima. With a rope fastened to her back leg, she walked off quite unconcernedly, without a backward glance. He is coming for Clarabella on Friday, as she will be dried off by then.

Friday 1st
Old Binks came over and took Clarabella. She is the last to go and followed him down the road at the end of a halter. So, gently, my dear sweet patient Clarabella walked out of my life. There were tears in my eyes as I watched them disappearing round the bend. I can only feel glad that she will not be lonely any more but will have plenty of company. Now I am left with only a few hens, most uninteresting, but I still have the dogs and the cats and have to make the best of them.

Tuesday 5th
Bracken Hill is like the land of the lost. Both Granny and I feel it. She even misses the film stars on the wall. In spite of the lovely weather we are lonely without all the animals. To prevent my thinking about it, I started cleaning out all the

sheds thoroughly. Empty sheds! Silent sheds! We are going to have a wonderful summer this year, I can feel it in my bones, and we shan't be here to enjoy it. Completion day is the 14th, and then we shall be gone. I have taken all the wire up into the top field and the stakes too, ready for Old Binks to make our boundary fence when he has time. To make quite sure of the boundary, he came across and, together, we took a few stakes and a strand of wire and the hammer, and, enclosing the three Scots pines on our side, continued the old fence down into the Valley of Lost Horizons. The nettles are high again and the bracken comes up to our shoulders. Our fourteen acres of land in Yorkshire, the remnants of a great adventure.

The solicitor has now established that the boundary is, as I thought, the old stone wall. I feel very glad that I stood out for my rights all that time ago, but the victory has a hollow ring. One day, who knows, we may plant trees on the moor; I love trees.

Old Binks is having the hay this year. It will be a good crop as there are no rabbits. We have finished off the muckheap and spread it on the four acres. Now there remains only the packing up. I found two squirrel tails in the sideboard drawer, but I put them back in. Why? I don't know!

The hay is finished, the straw gone, the turnips and potatoes eaten and we have no surplus food, only just enough to feed the few remaining hens, almost back where we started. We even have to go across for milk again.

Granny feels almost as sad as I do, but we know it was inevitable and make the best of it. Even though we wouldn't have missed the experience, we just couldn't have faced it again.

Wednesday 13th
The removal van arrived early and the men took out the furniture, which, a year before, they had carried in. Cups of tea and sandwiches consumed, they were off down the road, then up to the gate and very precariously round the corner and on the way. Granny had stayed to see the furniture safely packed and now she, too, was ready to go. We settled her safely into the van, the stool was put in the back with her case

and possessions, and she was delivered safely back to Ida. Ida, I am sure, was very relieved to have Granny back where she could keep her eye on her as she had been more worried than we, during our imprisonment. I know Granny would not have missed it for the world, and what could I have done without her?

As one door shuts, another opens, they say. I suppose another phase is starting.

We are sleeping on the floor tonight with a minimum of bedclothes, in an empty echoing house. Our last night in Bracken Hill. There is a lovely moon and Kilburn, snuggled in the hollow of the hills, is lit by a silvery glow. It is a lovely sight. I shall always remember it like that.

Thursday 14th

After a picnic breakfast, we packed up the rest of our possessions, fed the few hens, put Wodgie in front with us and poor old Brutus, in the back, tied up so that he couldn't wander, on piles of sacks so that he wouldn't be more sick than necessary, said goodbye to the kittens, leaving them the rest of the milk, and set off for our new home. I shall miss my little Torty.

As we wound our way up the road, I turned to get a last glimpse of Bracken Hill. There, at the top of the bank, the three Scots pines, David's pride and joy, stood silhouetted against the sky, and my heart ached a little.

I am one year older and a hundred years wiser.

I shall never forget it – never! never! never!

We did go back to see Old Binks. Clarabella had produced a beautiful, almost white, heifer calf, which I was called upon to name. 'Katy', I called her. I saw Simon too; a very big boar with half his ear missing. He responded as ever to my scratching and lay down grunting contentedly. The bees were still in the box, prolific as ever. But it was different. They weren't mine any longer!

And here we are, in our little cottage – and – there are pigs at the bottom of our garden!